CW01475791

A GUIDE TO ṢALĀḤ

M. A. K. SAQIB

Ta-Ha Publishers Ltd.

First Edition 1983
Second Edition 1986
Third Revised Edition 2021

Published by:
Ta-Ha Publishers Ltd,
London, UK
Website: www.tahapublishers.com
E-mail: support@tahapublishers.com

Translated by: Ijaz Begum Saqib
Researched and edited by: Muhammad Abdul Karim Saqib
Third Edition edited by: Dr Abia Afsar-Siddiqui
Layout and Design by: DigitEaze Media
Cover Design by: Faiçal Mohamed Kasimi

A catalogue record of this book is available from the British Library

Paperback ISBN: 978 1 84200 096 0

Printed and bound by: Mega Basim, Turkey

CONTENTS

FOREWORD

There are many books dealing with the subject of ṣalāḥ in both Arabic and Urdu. Many of these books are well written and provide an informative and comprehensive view of how ṣalāḥ should be performed according to the teachings of Prophet Muhammad ﷺ. Unfortunately, there are very few books in English which deal with the subject in the same informative and comprehensive way. The books, which do exist, have three main disadvantages.

Firstly, literature concerning ṣalāḥ available in English is either so brief that it does not cover essential points in nearly enough detail, or it is so bulky and detailed that it becomes difficult to use it for quick reference and essential points may get lost in the unnecessary detail.

Secondly, the text of the ṣalāḥ lacks the quality of direct research from the sunnah of the Prophet Muhammad ﷺ. There are also books which contain material without any reference to the original sources.

Thirdly, the majority of books have been written according to the views held by certain schools of thought and for this reason some people hesitate to follow them.

Due to these weaknesses in existing literature in English, we felt that the need existed to produce a medium sized book on ṣalāḥ which would approach the subject according to the teachings of the Prophet Muhammad ﷺ. The Prophet ﷺ himself said:

"Pray as you have seen me praying."

Such a book needs to contain all the essential details of ṣalāḥ without being too bulky or complicated so that the reader can use it as a point of reference on a journey or at home.

It was also felt that a comprehensive book on ṣalāḥ in English would be useful for converts to Islam and for Muslim youth brought up in this country. Keeping in mind the needs of our brothers and sisters, every effort has been made to produce this book in simple and easy language.

During our research we sometimes found that differences occurred between established practices in various prayer books. In these circumstances we have referred to authentic hadiths of the Prophet Muhammad ﷺ so that the points can be clarified as much as possible. This was because, for a true Muslim, there is no greater proof for settling arguments than authentic hadiths and practices of Prophet Muhammad ﷺ.

O you who believe! Obey Allah and obey the Messenger (Muhammad) and those of you who are in authority; and if you have a dispute or disagreement in anything among yourselves, then refer it to Allah and His Messenger if you believe in Allah and the Last Day. Then that is better and more suitable for the final determination.
(Surah Nisa 4:59)

This verse explains about the basic principles and guidelines to deal with disputes and disagreements amongst the Muslims, if there are any.

We hope that Allah will accept this humble attempt because without His support and help we would never have been able to do this work.

Finally, we ask all our Muslim brothers and sisters to study the text and to strive to pray according to it. If anyone finds anything unacceptable or to be against the sunnah of the Prophet ﷺ, we would be grateful if they would inform us.

Muhammad Abdul Karim Saqib

TRANSLITERATION SYSTEM

In transliterating Arabic words, the following system of symbols has been used.

b	=	ب	z	=	ز	f	=	ف
t	=	ت	s	=	س	q	=	ق
th	=	ث	sh	=	ش	k	=	ك
j	=	ج	ṣ	=	ص	l	=	ل
ḥ	=	ح	ḍ	=	ض	m	=	م
kh	=	خ	ṭ	=	ط	n	=	ن
d	=	د	ẓ	=	ظ	h	=	ه
dh	=	ذ	ʻ	=	ع	w	=	و
r	=	ر	gh	=	غ	y	=	ي

A macron over an Arabic vowel indicates a lengthening of that vowel.

SALUTATIONS

ﷺ Sallallāhu ʻalayhi wa sallam (Peace and Blessings of Allah be upon him)

رضي الله عنه رضي الله عنهم رضي الله عنها Raḍiallāhu ʻanhū/anhum/anhā (May Allah be Pleased with him/them/her)

عليه السلام Alayhis salām (Peace be upon him)

سبحانه وتعالى Subḥānahū wa taʻāla (Glory be to Allah, Most High)

CHAPTER 1: PURIFICATION

THE IMPORTANCE OF PURIFICATION

The first precondition to be fulfilled before praying ṣalāḥ is ritual purification. The process of ritual purification is known as wuḍū, which will be described in full in this chapter. If a person does not have wuḍū, then their ṣalāḥ will not be valid, so it is extremely important for wuḍū to be done correctly and properly. If the wuḍū is not done correctly, then it will not be valid and thus, the ṣalāḥ will also not be valid.

BEFORE DOING WUḌŪ

If someone needs to go to the toilet, they should use the toilet and do istanja (washing the private parts) before doing wuḍū (ablution).

SIWĀK (TOOTH-STICK)

It is good practice to clean the teeth with a tooth-stick or a toothbrush before performing wuḍū. In this way, one can avoid many diseases which are caused by unclean teeth. As mentioned in the hadith, Aishah ﵂ reported Allah's Messenger ﷺ as saying:

Evidence
"The use of a tooth-stick is a means of purifying the mouth and is pleasing to the Lord as well." (Ahmad, Darimi and Nisai)

Prophet Muhammad ﷺ also said:

Evidence
"If I had not felt that it would be difficult for my people, I would have ordered them to use a tooth stick with every prayer (that is, before doing each wuḍū)." (Ahmad, Malik, Nisai and Ibn Khuzaimah)

So, Muslims should always try to fulfil this wish of our Prophet ﷺ.

MAKING INTENTION FOR WUḌŪ (NIYAH)

Before starting the actions of wuḍū, it is necessary to make niyah (intention). Niyah should be made that the act of performing wuḍū is for the purpose of purity only. Niyah should be made in the heart because it is an action of the heart and not of the tongue. Niyah by words is not approved by Prophet Muhammad ﷺ.

Then start the wuḍū by saying:

Arabic	بِسْمِ ٱللَّهِ ٱلرَّحْمَٰنِ ٱلرَّحِيمِ
Transliteration	Bismillāhir raḥmān nir raḥeem
Translation	In the name of Allah, Most Gracious, Most Merciful

ACTIONS FOR PERFORMING WUḌŪ

1. Wash the hands up to the wrist making sure that no part of the hands is left dry.
2. Rinse the mouth taking up water with the right hand.
3. Clean the nose: sniff water up from the right palm and then eject water with the left hand.
4. Wash the face, from ear to ear and forehead to chin, making sure that no part of the face is left dry.
5. Wash the forearms (right forearm first) up to the elbows, making sure that no part of them is left dry.
6. Rub the head: wet your fingers and then wipe your head with them, starting from the forehead, taking them to the nape of the neck and then bring them back to the forehead.

7. Clean the ears by inserting the tips of the index fingers wetted with water into the ears, twist them around the folds of the ears then pass the thumb behind the ears from the bottom, upwards.

8. Wash the feet (right foot first) up to the ankles making sure that no parts of the feet are left dry, especially in between the toes. *

* Rubbing the socks with wet hands (masa') instead of washing the feet is allowed, provided that the socks have been put on after performing an ablution, including washing the feet. This is allowed for twenty-four hours from the time the first masa' is done, and for three days, if the person is on a journey. After this time, the feet must be washed. Similarly, if there is a wound on any part of the body which has to be washed in ablution, and if washing that particular part is likely to cause harm, it is permissible to wipe the dressing of the wound with a wet hand.

Evidence
Mughira bin Shu'bah said: "The Prophet ﷺ performed ablution and wiped over his socks and his sandals." (Ahmad, Tirmidhi, Abu Dawud and Ibn Majah)

Each detail of ablution has been performed by Prophet Muhammad ﷺ once, twice or three times (except rubbing of the head and cleaning of the ears, i.e. actions 6 and 7 should only be done once). Since all the above methods meet the Prophet's ﷺ approval, we can perform ablution by doing the actions once, twice or three times, provided that no part has been left dry.

Evidence
Amr bin Shu'aib quoting his father on the authority of his grandfather narrated that Prophet Muhammad ﷺ said: "If anyone performs actions of ablution more than three times, he has done wrong, transgressed, and done wickedly." (Nisai and Ibn Majah)

DU‘Ā AT THE END OF WUḌŪ

Arabic	أَشْهَدُ أَنْ لَا إِلَهَ إِلَّا اللَّهُ وَحْدَهُ لَا شَرِيكَ لَهُ، وَأَشْهَدُ أَنَّ مُحَمَّدًا عَبْدُهُ وَرَسُولُهُ
Transliteration	Ash hadu an lā ilāha illallāhu waḥdahū la shareeka lahū wa ash hadu anna Muḥammadan ‘abduhū wa rasuluhū
Translation	I testify that there is no deity except Allah alone. He is One and has no partner, and I testify that Muhammad ﷺ is His servant and Messenger. (Muslim)

Arabic	اَللَّهُمَّ اجْعَلْنِي مِنَ التَّوَّابِينَ وَاجْعَلْنِي مِنَ الْمُتَطَهِّرِينَ
Transliteration	Allah hum-maj ‘alnee minat taw-wabeena waj ‘alnee minal mutaṭah-hireen
Translation	O Allah! Make me among those who are penitent and make me among those who are purified. (Tirmidhi)

TAYAMMUM (DRY ABLUTION)

In circumstances when water cannot be found, or just enough is available for drinking, or it is injurious to health: in such situations, tayammum (dry ablution) can be performed. The procedure below is given according to Qur’an and hadith:

Evidence
"And if you do not find any water, then take clean earth (or sand) and rub it on your face and hands. Allah does not wish to put you in difficulty, but He wants to make you clean, and to complete His favour unto you, so you should be grateful to Him." (Surat al Ma'idah 5:6)

(The permission to use sand for this purpose is allowed in the Qur'an.)

PROCEDURE FOR TAYAMMUM

1. Make niyah in the heart.
2. Begin with the name of Allah.
3. Strike both palms of hand on clean sand, dust or anything containing these, e.g. a wall or stone etc.
4. Blow into the palms and pass the palms of both hands over the face once and then rub your right hand with the left palm and left hand with the right palm. (Bukhari and Muslim)
5. Finish with the same du'ā as given at the end of wuḍū.

Note: Other procedures include the forearms and shoulders as well as armpits. These have been transmitted by reputable scholars but the most preferable and authentic method is that given above.

CHAPTER 2: BEFORE ṢALĀḤ

TIME OF ṢALĀḤ

Each ṣalāḥ must be offered at or during its proper time. No ṣalāḥ can be offered before its time. There are five obligatory (fard) ṣalāḥs in a day:

Fajr Prayer

The time for Fajr, or the morning prayer, starts at dawn and ends at sunrise.

Ẓuhr Prayer

The time for Ẓuhr, or the early afternoon prayer, starts when the sun begins to decline from its zenith (highest point) and ends when the size of an object's shadow is equal to the size of the object.

Evidence
Jabir bin Abdullah ﷺ narrated: "The Angel Jibreel came to Prophet Muhammad ﷺ and said to him 'Stand up and pray Ẓuhr.' So, the Messenger of Allah ﷺ prayed Ẓuhr when the sun had declined from its zenith. Then the Angel Jibreel came again at the time of 'Asr and said 'Stand up and pray 'Asr.' Then Prophet Muhammad ﷺ prayed 'Asr when the shadow of everything was equal to itself. Then Jibreel came the next day to Prophet Muhammad ﷺ and said 'Stand up and pray Ẓuhr.' Then Prophet Muhammad ﷺ prayed Ẓuhr when the shadow of everything was equal to itself. Then Jibreel came again at 'Asr time and said 'Stand up and pray 'Asr.' Then he prayed 'Asr when the shadow of everything was twice its length. Then Jibreel said (after praying ten prayers with Prophet Muhammad ﷺ) 'The time of prayer is in between these two times.'" (Ahmad, Nisai, Tirmidhi and Bukhari remarked that this is the most authentic hadith giving the times of prayer)

We find that many books on ṣalāḥ state the ending time of the Ẓuhr prayer and the starting time of the 'Asr prayer when the shadow of something is twice itself, especially the books which are written by the followers of the Hanafi school of thought. But this contradicts the above hadith, as on the first day Jibreel asked Prophet Muhammad ﷺ to pray 'Asr when the shadow of everything was equal to itself. This means that was the end time of Ẓuhr prayer and we already know that all the 'ulamā (scholars) of the Muslim Ummah agree unanimously that no prayer can be offered before its time.

Imam Abu Hanifah is reported to have changed his opinion before he passed away, and prayed his 'Asr prayer according to the time stated in this hadith. His two students, Imam Abu Yusuf and Imam Muhammad, used to give fatawā (legal verdicts) for the time of 'Asr prayer according to this hadith, too. (Fatawa Azeeziah and Fatawa Rasheediah)

'Asr Prayer

The time for 'Asr, or the late afternoon prayer, starts when the shadow of something is equal to itself and ends just before sunset.

It is better to offer the 'Asr prayer before the sun becomes yellow, because even though it is allowed to offer the prayer at this time, the Prophet ﷺ disliked Muslims to delay 'Asr prayer up to this time. He remarked that the munāfiq (hyprocrite) offered his prayer at this time.

Maghrib Prayer

The time for Maghrib, or the sunset prayer, starts just after sunset and ends when twilight has disappeared.

'Isha Prayer

The time for 'Isha, or the night prayer, starts from the disappearance of twilight and ends just before midnight.

It is preferable to offer this prayer before midnight but it can be offered right up to the break of dawn.

Note: In countries where, due to cloudy weather, the sun is not always visible, it is advisable to follow printed calendars giving the accurate time of each prayer.

Forbidden Times of Prayer

Evidence
Uqbah bin Amir ﷺ said: "There were three times at which Allah's Messenger ﷺ used to forbid us to pray or bury our dead: (i) When the sun began to rise until it was fully up; (ii) When the sun was at its height at midday till it passed the meridian; (iii) When the sun drew near to setting till it had set." (Muslim)

Forbidden Times for Nafl (Extra) Prayer

Evidence
Abu Sa'id al Khudri ﷺ reported Allah's Messenger ﷺ as saying: "No prayer is to be offered after the Fajr prayer until the sun rises or after the 'Asr prayer until the sun sets." (Bukhari and Muslim)

Only nafl prayer is forbidden at these times but a missed fard prayer can be offered. Most of the 'ulamā of the Muslim Ummah allow the offering of missed fard prayer after Fajr and 'Asr because of the following hadith:

Evidence
Prophet Muhammad ﷺ said: "Who has forgotten the prayer he should pray it whenever he remembers it." (Bukhari and Muslim)

A nafl prayer cannot be offered once the iqāmah for fard prayer has been said:

Evidence
Abu Hurairah ﷛ narrated that the Messenger of Allah ﷺ said: "When the iqāmah has been said then there is no prayer valid (nafl or sunnah) except the fard prayer for which the iqāmah was said." (Ahmad and Muslim)

It is seen in practice that many people continue with the sunnah prayer even though the iqāmah has been said for the fard prayer especially in the Fajr prayer. They feel that the two rak'ahs sunnah of Fajr can only be offered before the fard. This practice is against congregation philosophy, discipline of jamā'at (congregation), and a clear violation of hadith. They should offer two rak'ahs sunnah of Fajr immediately after the fard or after sunrise. Both ways are authentic and proven from the Prophet ﷺ.

Evidence
Abu Hurairah ﷛ narrated that the Messenger of Allah ﷺ said that anyone who did not offer two rak'ahs sunnah of the Fajr prayer until the sunrise he should offer them after sunrise. (Baihaqi)

If a person misses two rak'ahs sunnah of the Fajr prayer because the jamā'at has already started (for the Fajr prayer), he should join the jamā'at and offer two rak'ahs sunnah of the Fajr immediately after the fard of the Fajr.

Evidence
Qais bin Umar ﷛ narrated that he went to pray Fajr (in the mosque) and found the Prophet ﷺ praying fard of Fajr. He (Qais bin Umar) did not offer two rak'ahs sunnah of Fajr, but joined the fard prayer with the Prophet ﷺ. After finishing the fard prayer of the Fajr, he stood up and offered two rak'ahs sunnah of the Fajr (which he had missed). Then the Prophet ﷺ came across to him and said, "What kind of prayer was this?" Qais bin Umar ﷛ told him everything. So, the Prophet ﷺ kept silent and did not say anything. (Ahmad, Ibn Khuzaimah, Ibn Hibban, Abu Dawud, Ibn Majah and Tirmidhi)

All the Muslim 'ulamā, fuqahā (jurists) and muḥadditheen (scholars of hadith) agree with the principle that whenever Prophet Muhammad ﷺ keeps quiet about a matter or an action done in his presence, then it is approved.

PLACE FOR ṢALĀḤ

A place or a building which is used for the purpose of worship and prayer is called a masjid (mosque).

Evidence
Abu Hurairah ؓ tells us that the Messenger of Allah ﷺ said: "...all the earth has been rendered for the Muslims, a mosque (pure and clean), and I am sent to all the universe as a Prophet and the chain of Prophethood has been completed by me (that is, Prophet Muhammad ﷺ is the last of the Prophets)." (Muslim)

This means that wherever a Muslim might be, he can offer his prayer, but the reward of a prayer offered in a mosque is far greater than that offered in an ordinary place. The following points should be noted when choosing a place of prayer:

(a) The place should be clean and pure. Ṣalāḥ in a dirty, filthy and impure place such as a rubbish tip, slaughter house, bathing place and a camel pen is forbidden. (Tirmidhi, Ibn Majah and Abd bin Humaid)
(b) The place should be free from danger. The danger could be because of someone or something which may disturb the worshipper.
(c) A prayer place where the worshipper might hinder movement of others should be avoided, e.g. busy pavements, public roadways, etc.
(d) It is forbidden to pray on the roof of Baitullah (the Kā'bah). (Ibn Majah and Abd bin Humaid)
(e) It is forbidden to pray on top of or facing towards a grave. (Ahmad and Muslim)

DRESS FOR ṢALĀḤ

Men

(i) The dress for men should be such that it covers them from the navel to the knees, at least.
(ii) The shoulders should not be left uncovered.
(iii) Ṣalāḥ can be prayed in one garment, if it covers the body from the navel to the knees as well as the shoulders.

Evidence
"None of you must pray in a single garment of which no part comes over the shoulder." (Bukhari and Muslim)

Women

The dress of the woman should be such that it covers her whole body from head to foot leaving only the face and the hands uncovered. A prayer offered in transparent clothing is not valid. Also, tight fitting clothing which shows the shape of the body should be avoided.

TYPES OF ṢALĀḤ

a) Fard or Obligatory Ṣalāḥ: Fard prayer is an obligatory prayer. Every believer is ordered by Allah ﷻ to offer five obligatory prayers in a day. Failure to observe any one of the five obligatory prayers is a serious and punishable sin.
b) The other prayers can be divided into three categories: i) Sunnah Mu'akkadah (Recommended): These are those which are emphasised by the Prophet ﷺ and were offered regularly by him before or after the fard prayer.
ii) Sunnah Ghair Mu'akkadah (Optional): These were offered only occasionally by Prophet Muhammad ﷺ.

iii) Nafl Prayer (Extra): This is an extra prayer. There is a reward for praying it and no sin for leaving it. It can be offered at any isolated instance according to the time and capacity of the believer. Prophet Muhammad ﷺ encouraged the believers to pray nafl to help make up for any minor omissions or other defects in the obligatory prayer.

Number of Rak'ahs for the Five Obligatory Prayers

i) Fajr Prayer

2 rak'ahs sunnat mu'akkadah
2 rak'ahs fard

ii) Ẓuhr Prayer

2 or 4 rak'ahs sunnat mu'akkadah
4 rak'ahs fard
2 rak'ahs sunnat mu'akkadah plus an unspecified number of nafl as time and capacity allows

Evidence
Ibn Umar ؓ said: "I prayed alone with Allah's Messenger ﷺ two rak'ahs before and two rak'ahs after the Ẓuhr prayer." (Bukhari and Muslim)

It is a familiar practice to offer four rak'ahs sunnah before Ẓuhr prayer, but this hadith proves that two rak'ahs sunnah before the Ẓuhr prayer is also allowed.

iii) 'Asr Prayer

2 or 4 rak'ahs sunnat ghair mu'akkadah
4 rak'ahs fard

Evidence
Ali ﷺ said: "Allah's Messenger ﷺ used to pray four rak'ahs before 'Asr prayer separating them with a salutation..." (Tirmidhi)
Another hadith narrated by Ali ﷺ states: "Allah's Messenger ﷺ used to pray two rak'ahs before 'Asr prayer." (Abu Dawud)

iv) Maghrib Prayer

2 rak'ahs nafl
3 rak'ahs fard
2 rak'ahs sunnat mu'akkadah plus an unspecified number of nafl as time and capacity allows

Evidence
Abdullah bin Mughaffal reported the Prophet ﷺ as saying: "Pray before the Maghrib prayer" adding when saying it the third time "This applies to those who wish to do so." (Bukhari and Muslim)

This was because he did not wish people to treat it as a recommended sunnah. Some people forbid this and others find it very strange if they see a person offer two rak'ahs nafl before Maghrib. However, two rak'ahs nafl after sunset and before the Maghrib prayer are allowed for those who wish to pray them, the proof being the above hadith.

v) 'Isha Prayer

An unspecified number of nafl rak'ahs according to the time and capacity
4 rak'ahs fard
2 rak'ahs sunnat mu'akkadah plus an unspecified number of nafl as time and capacity allows and 3 Witr

Some people insist very emphatically upon the offering of four rak'ahs optional sunnah before the 'Isha prayer but during our entire research, we could not find a single proof, any practice or order from Prophet Muhammad ﷺ or his Companions to justify this claim. Certainly it is allowed to pray nafl while waiting for the jamā'at.

Evidence
Abdullah bin Mughsil ؓ reported that indeed Prophet Muhammad ﷺ said that between every two adhāns there is nafl prayer, between every two adhāns there is nafl prayer, adding for the third time, for him who wishes to pray. (Ahmad, Tirmidhi and Nisai)
Abdullah bin Zubair ؓ also narrated that the Prophet ﷺ said that there is not any obligatory prayer unless there are two rak'ahs nafl prayer before it. (Ibn Hibban)

Note: These hadiths prove that two rak'ahs of nafl prayer can be offered according to the time and capacity of a person before every fard prayer including Maghrib and 'Isha prayer, and between every adhān and iqāmah.

Some people offer two rak'ahs nafl after the Witr prayer. However, there is an authentic hadith which states that the Witr prayer should be offered after all the nafl which a person wishes to pray have been offered.

Evidence
Ibn Umar ؓ reported that the Messenger of Allah ﷺ said: "Make Witr as the last prayer of your night prayer." (Mishkat)

CHAPTER 3: THE ADHĀN AND IQĀMAH

ADHĀN AND IQĀMAH

In all Muslim countries, the adhān is called aloud five times a day and you must have heard it. Have you ever wondered how it started?

The Story of Adhān

When the Muslims migrated from Makkah to Madinah, they used to agree about a fixed time for the congregational prayer. However, they found it difficult to remember the time fixed for the prayer sometimes, especially when they were busy doing their work.

One day, Prophet Muhammad ﷺ and the Muslims discussed the matter of calling the people for the congregational prayer at the exact time. Some of the believers suggested the use of something like the bell of the Christians, others suggested the use of a horn like that of the Jews, but Umar ؓ suggested sending someone to announce the prayer. Then Allah's Messenger ﷺ appointed Bilal bin Rabah ؓ to call the people to prayer. But it seems through the study of hadith that the method was not satisfactory. Then Prophet Muhammad ﷺ agreed to use a naqūs (a conch), something like the bell of the Christians but he was not happy to use it because of its similarity with the Christians.

After Prophet Muhammad ﷺ had ordered a bell to be made so that it could be struck to gather the people to prayer; on that same day a Companion, Abdullah bin Zaid bin Abd Rabbihi ؓ, said,

> "I was sleeping when I saw a man carrying a naqūs in his hands, and I said, 'Servant of Allah, will you sell this to me?' When he asked what I would do with it? I replied that we would use it to call the people to prayer. He said, 'Shall I not guide you to something better than that?' I replied, 'Certainly.' So, he told me to say:

'Allāhu Akbar, Allāhu Akbar, Allāhu Akbar, Allāhu Akbar, Ash hadu an lā ilāha illallāh, Ash hadu an lā ilāha illallāh, Ash hadu anna Muḥammadar rasūlallah, Ash hadu anna Muḥammadar rasūlallah, Ḥayya 'alas ṣalāḥ, Ḥayya 'alas ṣalāḥ, Ḥayya 'alal falāḥ, Ḥayya 'alal falāḥ, Allāhu Akbar, Allāhu Akbar, Lā ilāha illallāh.'

After the adhān the stranger kept quiet for a while and then said, 'When the congregation is ready you should say, Allāhu Akbar, Allāhu Akbar, Ash hadu an lā ilāha illallāh, Ash hadu anna Muḥammadar rasūlallah, Ḥayya 'alas ṣalāḥ, Ḥayya 'alal falāḥ, Qad qāma tis ṣālaḥ, Qad qāma tis ṣalāḥ, Allāhu Akbar, Allāhu Akbar, Lā ilāha illallāh.'

When I told Allah's Messenger ﷺ in the morning what I had seen, he said, 'It is a true vision, Insha'Allah, so get up along with Bilal, and when you have taught him what you have seen let him use it in making the call to prayer, for he has a stronger voice than you have.'

So, I got up along with Bilal and began to teach it to him and he used it in making the call to prayer. Umar bin al-Khattab ؓ heard this when he was in his house and he came out trailing his cloak and said, 'Messenger of Allah ﷺ, by Him Who has sent you with the truth, I have seen the same kind of thing as has been revealed.' To this Allah's Messenger ﷺ replied, 'Praise be to Allah!'" (Darimi, Ahmad, Ibn Majah, Ibn Khuzaimah and Tirmidhi)

So, from that day on to the present day, the adhān is called to gather the people for the congregational prayer.

The Muadhdhin

A person who calls people for the congregational prayer is called a muadhdhin. Before saying the adhān he should stand facing towards the Qiblah. The Qiblah is pointing in the direction of the Kā'bah (the most sacred mosque of Islam, in Makkah, Saudi Arabia.) He should raise his hands to his ears putting the tips of forefingers into his ears and call in a loud voice. When he says Ḥayya 'alas ṣalāḥ he should turn his face to the right and when he says Ḥayya 'alal falāḥ he should turn his face to the left.

Text of the Adhān

Arabic	اَللّٰهُ أَكْبَرُ، اَللّٰهُ أَكْبَرُ ، اَللّٰهُ أَكْبَرُ ، اَللّٰهُ أَكْبَرُ أَشْهَدُ أَنْ لَا إِلَهَ إِلَّا اللّٰهُ أَشْهَدُ أَنْ لَا إِلَهَ إِلَّا اللّٰهُ أَشْهَدُ أَنَّ مُحَمَّدًا رَسُولُ اللّٰهِ أَشْهَدُ أَنَّ مُحَمَّدًا رَّسُولُ اللّٰهِ حَيَّ عَلَى الصَّلَاةِ ، حَيَّ عَلَى الصَّلَاةِ حَيَّ عَلَى الْفَلَاحِ ، حَيَّ عَلَى الْفَلَاحِ اَللّٰهُ أَكْبَرُ ، اَللّٰهُ أَكْبَرُ لَا إِلَهَ إِلَّا اللّٰهُ
Transliteration	Allāhu Akbar, Allāhu Akbar, Allāhu Akbar, Allāhu Akbar, Ash hadu an lā ilāha illallāh, Ash hadu an lā ilāha illallāh, Ash hadu anna Muḥammadar rasūlallah, Ash hadu anna Muḥammadar rasūlallah Ḥayya ‘alas ṣalāḥ, Ḥayya ‘alas ṣalāḥ Ḥayya ‘alal falāḥ, Ḥayya ‘alal falāḥ Allāhu Akbar, Allāhu Akbar Lā ilāha illallāh

Translation	Allah is the greatest, Allah is the greatest, Allah is the greatest, Allah is the greatest, I bear witness that there is no deity but Allah, I bear witness that there is no deity but Allah, I bear witness that Muhammad ﷺ is the Messenger of Allah, I bear witness that Muhammad ﷺ is the Messenger of Allah, Come to prayer, Come to prayer Come to your good, Come to your good, Allah is the greatest, Allah is the greatest, There is no deity but Allah

Adhān for Fajr

An additional phrase is included twice in the adhān for the Fajr prayer after the second Ḥayya 'alal falāḥ:

Arabic	اَلصَّلَاةُ خَيْرٌ مِنَ النَّوْمِ ، اَلصَّلَاةُ خَيْرٌ مِنَ النَّوْمِ
Transliteration	As ṣalātu khayrum minan nawm, As ṣalātu khayrum minan nawm
Translation	Prayer is better than sleep, Prayer is better than sleep

Listening to the Adhān

1) When the believers hear the adhān they should listen to it in silence and repeat each phrase of the adhān immediately after the muadhdhin has finished saying the phrase.
2) When the muadhdhin says: Ḥayya 'alas ṣalāḥ and Ḥayya 'alal falāḥ the listener should say in reply:

Arabic	لا حَوْلَ وَلا قُوَّةَ إِلا بِاللهِ
Transliteration	Lā ḥawla walā qūwwata illā billāh
Translation	There is no might nor power except with Allah

3) When the adhān has been completed, the listener and the muadhdhin recite durūd unto Prophet Muhammad ﷺ followed by a du'ā.

Durūd After the Adhān

Arabic	اَللّٰهُمَّ صَلِّ عَلٰی مُحَمَّدٍ وَّعَلٰی اٰلِ مُحَمَّدٍ كَمَا صَلَّيْتَ عَلٰی اِبْرَاهِيْمَ وَعَلٰی اٰلِ اِبْرَاهِيْمَ اِنَّكَ حَمِيْدٌ مَّجِيْدٌ اَللّٰهُمَّ بَارِكْ عَلٰی مُحَمَّدٍ وَّعَلٰی اٰلِ مُحَمَّدٍ كَمَا بَارَكْتَ عَلٰی اِبْرَاهِيْمَ وَعَلٰی اٰلِ اِبْرَاهِيْمَ اِنَّكَ حَمِيْدٌ مَّجِيْدٌ
Transliteration	Allah humma ṣalli 'alā Muḥammadin wa 'alā āli Muḥammadin, kamā ṣallayta 'alā Ibraheema wa 'alā āli Ibraheema innaka ḥameedum Majeed. Allah humma bārik 'alā Muḥammadin wa 'alā āli Muḥammadin kama bārakta 'alā Ibraheema wa 'alā āli Ibraheema innaka ḥameedum majeed

Translation	O Allah! Let Your peace come upon Muhammad ﷺ and the family of Muhammad ﷺ, as You have sent peace upon Ibrahim عليه السلام and the family of Ibrahim عليه السلام, Truly You are praiseworthy and glorious. O Allah! Bless Muhammad ﷺ and the family of Muhammad ﷺ, as You have blessed Ibrahim عليه السلام and the family of Ibrahim عليه السلام, Truly You are praiseworthy and glorious

DU'Ā OF ADHĀN

Arabic	اللَّهُمَّ رَبَّ هَذِهِ الدَّعْوَةِ التَّامَّةِ وَالصَّلاَةِ الْقَائِمَةِ آتِ مُحَمَّدًا نِالْوَسِيلَةَ وَالْفَضِيلَةَ وَابْعَثْهُ مَقَامًا مَحْمُودًا نِالَّذِي وَعَدْتَهُ
Transliteration	Allah humma rabba hādhi hid-da'wa-tit tāmmati was ṣalātil qā'imati āti Muḥammada nil waseelata wal faḍeelata wab 'athhu maqāmam maḥmūda nil ladhee wa'ad tahū
Translation	O Allah! Lord of this complete prayer of ours. By the blessing of it, give Muhammad ﷺ his eternal rights of intercessions, distinction and highest class (in paradise) and raise him to the promised rank You have promised him

Evidence
Jabir ؓ reported Allah's Messenger ﷺ as saying: "If anyone says upon hearing the adhān 'O Allah, Lord of this perfect call and of the prayer which is established for all time grant Muhammad ﷺ the waseela and excellency and raise him up in a praiseworthy position which you have promised' he will be assured of my intercession." (Bukhari)

IQĀMAH

Iqāmah is the second call to prayer and is uttered immediately before the beginning of the obligatory prayer offered with congregation.

Text of Iqāmah

Arabic	اَللّٰهُ أَكْبَرُ ، اللّٰهُ أَكْبَرُ أَشْهَدُ أَنْ لَا إِلٰهَ إِلَّا اللّٰهُ أَشْهَدُ أَنَّ مُحَمَّدً رَّسُولُ اللّٰهِ حَيَّ عَلَى الصَّلَاةِ ، حَيَّ عَلَي الْفَلَاحِ قَدْ قَامَتِ الصَّلَاةُ ، قَدْ قَامَتِ الصَّلَاةُ اَللّٰهُ أَكْبَرُ ، اَللّٰهُ أَكْبَرُ لَا إِلٰهَ إِلَّا اللّٰهُ
Transliteration	Allāhu Akbar, Allāhu Akbar, Ash hadu an lā ilāha illallāh, Ash hadu anna Muḥammadar rasūlallah Ḥayya 'alas ṣalāḥ, Ḥayya 'alal falāḥ, Qad qāma tis ṣālaḥ, Qad qāma tis ṣalāḥ, Allāhu Akbar, Allāhu Akbar, Lā ilāha illallāh

Translation	Allah is the greatest, Allah is the greatest I bear witness that there is no deity but Allah, I bear witness that Muhammad ﷺ is the Messenger of Allah, Come to prayer, Come to your good The congregation is ready, The congregation is ready, Allah is the greatest, Allah is the greatest, There is no deity but Allah

This text of iqāmah is the same as that mentioned in the hadith of Abdullah bin Zaid bin Abd Rabbihi رضي الله عنه who was the first to have the vision about adhān.

CHAPTER 4: CONDUCT OF ṢALĀḤ

SUTRAH

Before a person starts to pray, they should place something at a short distance in front of themselves on the place where they prostrate (do sajdah). Such an object is called a sutrah and is used when the person is praying alone. A person passing in front of the person in prayer, should pass on the outside of the sutrah.

If someone is praying in congregation, then the imam acts as the sutrah. The imam, however, must have his own individual sutrah in front of him.

QIBLAH

Wherever a person is in the world, they should face towards the Qiblah when they are going to pray. Facing towards the Qiblah is a very important precondition in performing the prayer. However, if the person is in a place such as a desert, jungle, unknown strange city or a place where they do not know the direction of the Qiblah, they should try their best to find out the direction of Qiblah from others. However, if it is not possible, then they should use their judgement and face in a direction which they think is that of Qiblah and Allah ﷻ will accept their prayer.

It is important to start the prayer facing the direction of Qiblah and it does not matter if the direction changes during prayer, e.g. in a ship, a train or an aeroplane etc.

Note: Nowadays, a compass and other aids are available which give the direction of Qiblah. In strange places and aeroplanes, these are useful devices to possess.

INTENTION (NIYAH)

After facing the Qiblah, the person should make niyah (intention). The intention is made within the mind, so the person should think about the particular obligatory, optional or nafl prayer that they intend to perform.

The words of the niyah should not be uttered aloud, as this is not authentic or approved by the Prophet ﷺ.

THE COMPLETE GUIDE TO ṢALĀḤ

Takbeer Taḥrimah

After making niyah, the person should start the prayer by saying:

Arabic	اَللّٰهُ اَكْبَرُ
Transliteration	Allāhu Akbar
Translation	Allah is the Greatest

raising both of the hands to the shoulders, with fingers stretching to the earlobes. They should then fold the hands over the chest, right hand over left hand. This first Allāhu Akbar is called takbeer taḥrimah because after saying takbeer taḥrimah, every common and worldly action, talk or movement is forbidden. Throughout the prayer, the eyes of the worshipper should point to the spot where the forehead rests in sajdah.

Where Should the Hands be Folded and Placed After Saying Takbeer Taḥrimah?

Some people place their hands under the navel, others place them under the chest but there are hadiths which state that Prophet Muhammad ﷺ used to place his hands over his chest.

Evidence
Halb Ata'i رضي الله عنه reported: "I saw the Prophet ﷺ placing his right hand over his left hand over his chest." (Ahmad and Tirmidhi)
Wa'il bin Hajr رضي الله عنه said: "I prayed with Prophet Muhammad ﷺ and he put his right hand over his left hand over his chest." (Ibn Khuzaimah, Abu Dawud and Muslim)

There are some other narrations which state that some fuqahā used to place their hands under the chest but above the navel. Placing the hands in either of these positions is correct, but it is better to place them over the chest according to the practice of Prophet Muhammad ﷺ as mentioned in the above authentic hadiths.

Recitation Before Fātiḥah

There are several du'ās which Prophet Muhammad ﷺ used to recite before Sūrah Fātiḥah. We will mention one of them:

Arabic	اَللّٰهُمَّ بَاعِدْ بَيْنِي وَبَيْنَ خَطَايَایَ كَمَا بَاعَدْتَ بَيْنَ الْمَشْرِقِ وَالْمَغْرِبِ اَللّٰهُمَّ نَقِّنِي مِنَ الْخَطَايَا كَمَا يُنَقَّى الثَّوْبُ الأَبْيَضُ مِنَ الدَّنَسِ اَللّٰهُمَّ اغْسِلْ خَطَايَایَ بِالْمَاءِ وَالثَّلْجِ وَالْبَرَدِ
Transliteration	Allah humma bā'id baynee wa bayna khaṭāyāya kamā bā'adta baynal mashriqi wal maghribi, Allah humma naqqinee minal khaṭāyāya kamā yunaqqath thawbul abyaḍu minad danasi, Allah hum maghsil khaṭāyāya bil ma'i wath thalji wal baradi
Translation	O Allah! Set me apart from my sins as East and West are apart from each other. O Allah! Cleanse me of my sins as a white garment is cleansed from dirt after thorough washing. O Allah! Wash my sins away with water, snow and hail. (Bukhari and Muslim)

If a person does not know the du'ā just mentioned, then they should recite the following one. Umar ﷺ is reported to have used this du'ā after saying takbeer taḥrimah:

Arabic	سُبْحَانَكَ اللَّهُمَّ وَبِحَمْدِكَ وَتَبَارَكَ اسْمُكَ وَتَعَالَى جَدُّكَ وَلَا إِلَهَ غَيْرُكَ
Transliteration	Subhāna kallah humma wabi ḥamdika wa tabāra kasmuka wa ta'āla jadduka wa lā ilāha ghayruka
Translation	Glory be to You, O Allah, and all praises are due unto You and blessed is Your name and high is Your majesty and none is worthy of worship but You

A person can read both du'ās together or just one of them or any of the other du'ās which are approved by Prophet Muhammad ﷺ and there about seven of these. These du'ās can be found in different places in several books of hadith (Muslim, Tirmidhi, Musnad of Imam Ahmad, Abu Dawud, Darqutni, Nisai, Ibn Majah, Ibn Hibban and Muwatta Imam Malik). All of the seven du'ās can be read together before reading Sūrah Fātiḥah.

This recitation is called Du'ā al-Istiftaḥ which means 'du'ā of starting'. Du'ā al-Istiftaḥ should only be read in the first rak'ah.

Ta‘ahwudh

Then the person who is praying should say:

Arabic	أَعُوذُ بِاللهِ مِنَ الشَّيْطَانِ الرَّجِيمِ
Transliteration	A‘ūdhu billāhi minash shayṭā-nir rajeem
Translation	I seek Allah's protection from satan who is accursed

This should only be said in the first rak‘ah.

Tasmiah

Then the person who is praying should say:

Arabic	بِسْمِ ٱللَّهِ ٱلرَّحْمَٰنِ ٱلرَّحِيمِ
Transliteration	Bismillāh hir raḥmān nir raḥeem
Translation	In the name of Allah, the Most Gracious and the Most Merciful

This should be said in every rak‘ah before reciting Sūrah Fātiḥah.

Sūrah Fātiḥah

Then the person praying should recite Sūrah Fātiḥah:

Arabic	اَلْحَمْدُ لِلَّهِ رَبِّ الْعَالَمِينَ اَلرَّحْمَنِ الرَّحِيمِ مَالِكِ يَوْمِ الدِّينِ إِيَّاكَ نَعْبُدُ وَإِيَّاكَ نَسْتَعِينُ

	إِهْدِنَا الصِّرَاطَ الْمُسْتَقِيمَ صِرَاطَ الَّذِينَ أَنْعَمْتَ عَلَيْهِمْ غَيْرِ الْمَغْضُوبِ عَلَيْهِمْ وَلَا الضَّالِّينَ
Transliteration	Alḥamdu lillāhi rabbil ‘ālameen, Ar raḥmān nir raḥeem, Māliki yawmid deen, Iyyāka na‘budu wa iyyāka nasta‘een, Ihdinas ṣirāṭal mustaqeem, Ṣirāṭal ladheena an‘amta ‘alayhim, Ghayril maghḍūbi ‘alayhim, walad ḍālleen, (Āmeen)
Translation	Praise is only for Allah, Lord of the Universe, The Most Kind, the Most Merciful, The Master of the Day of Judgement, You alone we worship and to You alone we pray for help, Show us the Straight Way, the way of those whom You have blessed, who have not deserved Your anger, nor gone astray. (Ameen)

Reciting Fātiḥah is so important that Prophet Muhammad ﷺ said that no prayer is acceptable without the recitation of Fātiḥah.

Evidence
Ubadah bin Samit ؓ reported Allah’s Messenger ﷺ as saying: “There is no prayer acceptable without reciting Sūrah Fātiḥah.” (Bukhari, Muslim, Ahmad, Abu Dawud, Tirmidhi, Nisai and Ibn Majah)

Abu Hurairah ﷺ reported that the Messenger of Allah ﷺ was saying that anyone who prayed any kind of prayer and did not read in that Ummul Qur'ān (and in one version Fātiḥah-tal-Kitāb) his prayer will be deficient, will be deficient, will be deficient and not complete. (Bukhari, Muslim and Ahmad)
Abu Hurairah ﷺ reported the Messenger of Allah ﷺ as saying: "No prayer will benefit a person who did not read in it Sūrah Fātiḥah." (Ibn Khuzaimah, Ibn Hibban and Ahmad)

In the light of the above hadiths, we understand that Sūrah Fātiḥah must be recited or read in every rak'ah of any type of prayer.

Recitation of Sūrah Fātiḥah Behind an Imam

Some people are very confused whether they should or should not read Sūrah Fātiḥah while praying in congregation. But there should not be any confusion in this matter as the following hadiths very clearly answer the question.

Evidence
Ubadah bin Samit ﷺ said: "We were behind the Prophet ﷺ in the Fajr prayer, and he recited a passage from the Qur'an, but the recitation became difficult for him. Then when he finished, he said, 'Do you recite behind your imam?' We replied, 'Yes, Messenger of Allah.' Then the Messenger of Allah ﷺ said, 'Do not recite anything (behind the imam) except Fātiḥah-tal-Kitab (Sūrah Fātiḥah) because he who does not include it in his recitation in prayer his prayer is not valid.'" (Abu Dawud and Tirmidhi)
Abu Hurairah ﷺ reported that the Messenger of Allah ﷺ said: "If anyone observes prayer (ṣalāḥ) in which he does not read Ummul Qur'ān (Fātiḥah), it is deficient, it deficient, it is deficient, and not complete." It was said to Abu Hurairah ﷺ: "What should we do when we are behind an imam?" He (Abu Hurairah ﷺ) replied, "Read it in silence..." (Muslim)

Āmeen

It is sunnah to say āmeen when a person finishes recitation of Sūrah Fātiḥah in ṣalāḥ. If someone is praying alone, he should say āmeen in silence and if he is praying in congregation behind an imam then he should say āmeen fairly loudly when the imam finishes saying the last verse of Sūrah Fātiḥah. When saying āmeen, the voice of the whole congregation should resound at the same time.

There are many hadiths which prove that saying āmeen aloud is a sunnah of Prophet Muhammad ﷺ and it was the regular practice of the Companions. We will mention a few of these hadiths here:

Evidence
Naeem al Mujammar said: "I prayed behind Abu Hurairah ؓ. He recited Bismillāh hir raḥmān nir raḥeem, then he recited Sūrah Fātiḥah, and when he reached walad ḍālleen, he said āmeen after it and the people behind him said āmeen..." (Bukhari)
Abu Hurairah ؓ reported that the Messenger of Allah ﷺ said: "When the imam says Ghayril maghḍūbi 'alayhim walad ḍālleen, all of you should say āmeen because the angels say āmeen and the imam says āmeen. And whosoever says āmeen and his voice blends with that of the angels, he would be forgiven his sins." (Ahmed, Abu Dawud and Nisai)

Recitation After Sūrah Fātiḥah

It is sunnah for the person who is praying that they should read a sūrah from the Qur'an after Fātiḥah in the first two rak'ahs of the fard prayer. They can recite one or more sūrahs. Here are a few short sūrahs which can be recited:

1. Sūrah Ikhlās

Arabic	قُلْ هُوَ اللَّهُ أَحَدٌ اَللَّهُ الصَّمَدُ لَمْ يَلِدْ وَلَمْ يُولَدْ وَلَمْ يَكُن لَّهُ كُفُوًا أَحَدٌ
Transliteration	Qul huwal lāhu aḥad, Allāh hus ṣamad, Lam yalid walam yūlad, Walam yakullahū kufuwan aḥad
Translation	Say: He is Allah, the Only One, Allah helps and does not need help, He does not produce a child, and He was not born of anyone, There is no one equal to Him

2. Sūrah Falaq

Arabic	قُلْ أَعُوذُ بِرَبِّ الْفَلَقِ مِنْ شَرِّ مَا خَلَقَ وَمِنْ شَرِّ غَاسِقٍ إِذَا وَقَبَ وَمِنْ شَرِّ النَّفَّاثَاتِ فِي الْعُقَدِ وَمِنْ شَرِّ حَاسِدٍ إِذَا حَسَدَ
Transliteration	Qul a'ūdhu bi rabbil falaq, Min shar rimā khalaq, Wa min sharri ghāsiqin idhā waqab, Wa min sharrin naffāthāti fil 'uqad,

	Wa min sharri ḥāsidin idhā ḥasad
Translation	Say: I seek refuge in the Lord of the dawn, from the evil of all that He has created, and from the evil of the darkness of night when it falls, and from the evil of those (charmers) who blow into knots, and from the evil of the envier when he envies

3. Sūrah Nās

Arabic	قُلْ أَعُوذُ بِرَبِّ النَّاسِ مَلِكِ النَّاسِ إِلَٰهِ النَّاسِ مِنْ شَرِّ الْوَسْوَاسِ الْخَنَّاسِ اَلَّذِي يُوَسْوِسُ فِي صُدُورِ النَّاسِ مِنَ الْجِنَّةِ وَالنَّاسِ
Transliteration	Qul a'ūdhu bi rabbin nās, Malikin nās, ilāhin nās, Min shar ril waswāsil khannās, Alladhee yuwas wisu fee ṣudurin nās, Minal jinnati wannās
Translation	Say: I seek refuge in the Sustainer of mankind, the Owner of Mankind, Lord of Mankind, from the evil of the sneaking whisperer, who whispers in the hearts of mankind, (whether he be) from among jinns or mankind

Rukū' (Bowing)

Then the person praying should say Allāhu Akbar, raising both the hands to shoulder level with the palms facing outwards and fingers stretching to earlobes. They should then bend in rukū' so that the trunk (i.e. from head to hips) is perpendicular to the rest of the body (90 degrees). The hands should rest on the knees with the fingers spread apart, taking care that the arms do not touch the body. The person should be calm and composed in the rukū' posture and not hurry it. Then they should read at least three times:

Arabic	سُبْحَانَ رَبِّيَ الْعَظِيمِ
Transliteration	Subḥāna rabbi yal 'aẓeem
Translation	Glory be to my Lord Who is the greatest

This can be read 3, 5, 7, 9, 11 etc. times. There are some other du'ās which can be read with subḥāna rabbi yal 'aẓeem or instead of subḥāna rabbi yal 'aẓeem. Two of them are mentioned below:

Aishah ﵂ reported that the Messenger of Allah ﷺ mostly read the following du'ā in his rukū' and sajdah:

Arabic	سُبْحَانَكَ اللّٰهُمَّ رَبَّنَا وَبِحَمْدِكَ اَللّٰهُمَّ اغْفِرْلِي
Transliteration	Subḥāna kalla humma rabbanā wa biḥamdika, Allah hum maghfirlee
Translation	Glory be to You, O our Lord, and all praise be to You. O Allah! Forgive me. (Bukhari and Muslim)

Ali ﵁ reported that the Messenger of Allah ﷺ used to read the following du'ā in his rukū':

Arabic	اَللَّهُمَّ لَكَ رَكَعْتُ وَبِكَ آمَنْتُ ولَكَ أَسْلَمْتُ خَشَعَ لَكَ سَمْعِي وَبَصَرِي وَمُخِّي وَعَظْمِي وَعَصَبِي وَمَا اسْتَقَلَّت بِهِ قَدَمِي
Transliteration	Allah humma laka raka'tu wa bika āmantu wa laka aslamtu khasha'a, laka sam'ee wa baṣaree wa mukhkhee, wa 'aẓmee wa 'aṣabee wa mastaqallat bihee qadamee
Translation	O Allah! Unto You I have bowed, and in You I have believed, and to You I have submitted, My hearing, and my sight, and my mind, and my bones, and my tendons, and what my feet carry, are humbled before You. (Ahmad, Muslim and Abu Dawud)

Perfection of Rukū' and Sajdah

Evidence
Abi Masud al Badri ﷺ reported that the Messenger of Allah ﷺ said: "Allah does not consider the prayer of a man who does not straighten his back when bowing for rukū' and performing sajdah." (Ibn Khuzaimah, Ibn Hibban and Tabrani)
Abi Qatadah ﷺ reported that the Messenger of Allah ﷺ said: "The worst thief is one who steals in his prayer." Then the Companions asked, "How can someone steal from his prayer?" The Prophet ﷺ answered, "He does not complete his rukū' and sajdah with

perfection." Or he said, "He does not make his back straight in rukū' and sajdah." (Ahmad, Tabrani, Ibn Khuzaimah and Hakim)

These hadiths prove that rukū' and sajdah should be done calmly, slowly and perfectly, otherwise the ṣalāḥ of the person will be deficient.

Qawmah (Standing After Rukū')

After the perfect rukū', the person praying should raise their head from rukū' saying:

Arabic	سَمِعَ اللهُ لِمَنْ حَمِدَه
Transliteration	Sami' Allāh hu liman ḥamidah
Translation	Verily Allah listens to one who praises Him

and raise their hands up to the level of their shoulders with palms facing outwards and fingers stretched to the earlobes and then they should lower their hands to their sides. In the standing position, they should be erect so that the joints of the body go back in place. While in this position, they should recite one or all of the following du'ās as many times as they like.

Note: Some people get very annoyed when they see someone raising his hands while going into rukū' and again raising his hands while lifting his head from rukū'. There are, however, authentic hadiths which prove that Prophet Muhammad ﷺ used to raise his hands at the beginning of prayer before and after rukū' and when standing up for the third rak'ah.

Every single book of hadith like Bukhari, Muslim, Muwatta of Imam Malik, Abu Dawud, Tirmidhi, Nisai, Ibn Majah, Ibn Khuzaimah, Hakim, Ahmad, Shafa'i, Tabrani and Baihaqi mentions these hadiths. Nearly four hundred Companions also narrate this practice of Prophet Muhammad ﷺ.

So, there is not the slightest doubt that the raising of hands is sunnah and a person who practices this sunnah gets a greater reward than the person who does not practice it. However, even though the action is mentioned in the hadiths, all the ʻulamā agree that the prayer of a person who does not raise their hands is acceptable. Therefore, Muslims should not fight over this issue. If someone does not wish to raise their hands, they should not discourage others from doing so because it is not a major controversial point.

Duʻās in Qawmah

Arabic	رَبَّنَا لَكَ الْحَمْدُ
Transliteration	Rabbanā lakal ḥamd
Translation	O our Lord! All the praises be to You

or

Arabic	رَبَّنَا لَكَ الْحَمْدُ حَمْدًا كَثِيرًا طَيِّبًا مُبَارَكًا فِيهِ
Transliteration	Rabbanā lakal ḥamdu ḥamdan katheeran ṭayyiban mubārakan feeh
Translation	O our Lord! All praises be to You; very many, pure and blessed praises be to You

or

Abi Sa'id al Khudri ﷺ says that when the Messenger of Allah ﷺ used to say: Samiʻ Allāh hu liman ḥamida, he would follow it with:

Arabic	اَللَّهُمَّ رَبَّنَا لَكَ الْحَمْدُ مِلْءَ اَلسمَوَاتِ الْأَرْضِ مِنْ شَيْءٍ بعْدُ أَهْلَ اَلثنَاءِ وَالمَجْدِ أَحقُّ مَا قَالَ الْعَبْدُ وَكُلَنَا لَكَ عَبْدٌ اَللَّهُمَّ لَا مَانِعَ لِمَا أَعْطَيْتَ وَلَا مُعْطِيَ لِمَا مَنَعْتَ وَلَا يَنْفَعُ ذَا اَلْجَدِّ مِنْكَ اَلْجدّ

Transliteration	Allah humma rabbanā lakal ḥamdu mil as samawātil arḍi min shayin ba'du ah lath-thanāi wal majdi ahaq-quma qalal 'abdu wa kullanā laka 'abd, Allah humma la māni'a lima a'ṭayta walā mu'ṭiya lima mana'ta walā yanfa'u dhal jaddi minkal jad
Translation	O Allah, our Lord, all praises be to You, as much as they can fill the heavens and the earth and everything which You want to be filled after that. You deserve to be praised and glorified. You deserve more than what Your servant has said and all of us are Your slaves. Nobody can prevent whatever You want to give and nobody can give whatever You want to prevent and a person with high rank cannot benefit himself or another from his high rank against Your will. (Muslim, Ahmad and Abu Dawud)

First Sajdah (Prostration)

After the perfect qawmah, the person praying should move to perform sajdah saying Allāhu Akbar, putting palms downwards on the ground below the ears. The knees should be brought downwards on the ground. The fingers and toes should be pointing towards the Qiblah without spreading the fingers of the hands. During prostration, seven parts of the body should touch the ground:

(i) the forehead along with the tip of the nose
(ii and iii) both hands
(iv and v) both knees
(vi and vii) the bottom surface of the toes of both feet.

In this position, one should say:

Arabic	سُبْحَانَ رَبِّيَ الأَعْلَى
Transliteration	Subḥāna Rabbi yal a'la
Translation	O Allah! Glory be to You, the Most High

This should be said at least 3 times or 5, 7, 9, 11 etc. times. There are some other du'ās which can be read in the sajdah position.

Other Du'ās in Sajdah

Ali ﷺ said that the Messenger of Allah ﷺ used to say while doing sajdah:

Arabic	اَللّٰهُمَّ لَكَ سَجَدْتُ وَبِكَ آمَنْتُ وَلَكَ أَسْلَمْتُ سَجَدَ وَجْهِي لِلَّذِي خَلَقَهُ وَصَوَّرَهُ وَشَقَّ سَمْعَهُ وَبَصَرَهُ تَبَارَكَ اللهُ أَحْسَنُ الْخَالِقِينَ
Transliteration	Allah humma laka sajadtu wa bika āmantu wa laka aslamtu sajada wajhiya lil ladhee khalaqahū waṣawwarahū washaqqa sam'ahū wa baṣarahū, tabāra kallāhu aḥsanul khāliqeen
Translation	O Allah! For You I have prostrated and in You I have faith and unto You I have submitted; my forehead has prostrated in front of One Who created it and gave shape to it and made it perfectly. Then He gave the power of hearing and sight and blessed is Allah's name Who is the Perfect Creator. (Ahmad, Muslim)

Abu Hurairah ﷺ said that the Messenger of Allah ﷺ used to say in his sajdah:

Arabic	اَللّٰهُمَّ اغْفِرْلِي ذَنْبِي كُلَّهُ دِقَّهُ وَجِلَّهُ وَأَوَّلَهُ وَآخِرَهُ وَعَلانِيَتَهُ وَسِرَّهُ
Transliteration	Allah hummagh firlee dhanbee kullahū diqqahū wa jillahū wa awwalahū wa ākhirahū wa 'alāniyatahū wa sirahū
Translation	O Allah! Forgive all my sins, minor ones and major ones, ones I committed previously and ones I commit in the future, ones I commit openly and ones I commit secretly. (Muslim, Abu Dawud and Hakim)

There are some other du'ās which the Messenger of Allah ﷺ used to say in his sajdah but these are too long to mention here. They can be found in authentic books of hadith. It is not surprising that Prophet Muhammad ﷺ stayed in rukū' and sajdah for long intervals.

All of the authentically approved du'ās can be said with Subḥāna Rabbi yal a'la or on their own or altogether according to the time available and capacity of the person. In sajdah position, the worshipper is at their closest to Allah, hence, sajdah should be performed calmly and quietly without fidgeting and the worshipper should try and read as many du'ās as they possibly can.

Jalsah (Sitting Between Two Sajdah)

After performing one sajdah perfectly and calmly, the person praying should raise their head from sajdah saying Allāhu Akbar, bending the left foot and sitting on it while keeping the right foot propped up with its toes pointing towards the Qiblah. The palms of the hands should rest on the thighs and knees. The back should be straight so that the joints go back in place. It is sunnah to say the following du'ā while sitting in between the two sajdahs:

Arabic	اَللّٰهُمَّ اغْفِرْلِي وَارْحَمْنِي وَاجْبُرْنِي وَاهْدِنِي وَارْزُقْنِي
Transliteration	Allah humma maghfirlee, war ḥamnee waj burnee wah dinee, war zuqnee
Translation	O Allah! Forgive me, have mercy upon me, give me strength, guide me, give and grant me sustenance. (Abu Dawud)

The worshipper can say this du'ā once or as many times as they like.

Second Sajdah

Then the person should perform the second sajdah saying Allāhu Akbar and repeat what they did in the first sajdah.

Jalsah Istarāḥat (Sitting for Rest)

Then they should raise the head up saying Allāhu Akbar and sit for a short while as they did in jalsah. This is done before standing up for the second rak'ah.

Second Rak'ah

After standing up for the second rak'ah, the worshipper should fold the hands over the chest as they did in the first rak'ah and start the recitation by reading Bismillāh and Sūrah Fātiḥah followed by any passage or a sūrah of the Holy Qur'an. Then they should complete the second rak'ah in the manner of the first one.

While choosing a passage or sūrah for the recitation in the second or a subsequent rak'ah, the worshipper should observe the order in which they occur in the Holy Qur'an. Also, each sūrah should be shorter than the one recited before it. Hence, longer sūrahs are recited before shorter ones.

Tashahhud

After completing the last sajdah of the second rak'ah, the person should raise their head saying Allāhu Akbar. They should sit as they sat between the consecutive sajdah, putting the left hand on the left knee and the right hand on the right knee. The fist of the right hand is closed except for the index finger, which is protruded. It is protruded so that the right thumb is brought to the second division of the index finger. In this position, the person should read:

Arabic	اَلتَّحِيَّاتُ لِلّٰهِ وَالصَّلَوَاتُ والطَّيِّبَاتُ اَلسَّلَامُ عَلَيْكَ أَيُّهَا النَّبِيُّ وَرَحْمَةُ اللّٰهِ وَبَرَكَاتُهُ اَلسَّلَامُ عَلَيْنَا وَعَلَى عِبَادِ اللّٰهِ الصَّالِحِينَ أَشْهَدُ أَنْ لَا إِلٰهَ إِلَّا اللّٰهُ وَأَشْهَدُ أَنَّ مُحَمَّدًا عَبْدُهُ وَرَسُولُهُ
Transliteration	At taḥiyyātu lillāhi was ṣalawātu wat ṭayyibātu As salāmu 'alayka ayyuhan nabiyyu wa raḥmatullāhi wa barakātuhū As salāmu 'alayna wa 'ala 'ibadil lā his ṣaliḥeen, Ash hadu an lā ilāha illallāhu wa ash hadu anna Muḥammadan 'abduhu wa rasuluh
Translation	All compliments, all physical prayer and all monetary worship are for Allah Peace be upon you, O Prophet, and Allah's mercy and blessings Peace be on us and on all righteous slaves of Allah I bear witness that no one is worthy of worship except Allah and Muhammad is His slave and Messenger

While reading Ash hadu an lā ilāha illallāhu wa ash hadu anna Muḥammadan ‘abduhu wa rasuluh, a person should raise the index finger of the right hand slightly and return to its previous position after they have finished saying it.

A person praying two rak‘ahs only should continue to the next stage, which is ṣalāt ‘alan-Nabi (Durūd).

Standing Up for the Third Rak‘ah

If a person is praying three or four rak‘ahs, then they should stand up after tashahhud saying Allāhu Akbar and raising the hands as they did in takbeer taḥrimah. The third rak‘ah starts with the recitation of Bismillāhir raḥmān nir raḥeem followed by Sūrah Fātiḥah.

In the third or fourth rak‘ah of fard prayer recitation of Sūrah Fātiḥah is sufficient. There is no need to say another sūrah. But a person praying sunnah or nafl prayer can read another sūrah after Sūrah Fātiḥah. After this recitation, they should continue to complete the third rak‘ah (or fourth rak‘ah if they are praying four).

Last Rak‘ah

After the completion of the last rak‘ah, the worshipper should sit for tashahhud as described above (as they sat after praying two rak‘ahs). After tashahhud, they should read ṣalāt ‘alan-Nabi (Durūd) as follows:

Arabic	اَللّٰهُمَّ صَلِّ عَلٰى مُحَمَّدٍ وَّعَلٰٓى اٰلِ مُحَمَّدٍ كَمَا صَلَّيْتَ عَلٰٓى اِبْرَاهِيْمَ وَعَلٰى اٰلِ اِبْرَاهِيْمَ ، اِنَّکَ حَمِيْدٌ مَّجِيْدٌ اَللّٰهُمَّ بَارِکْ عَلٰى مُحَمَّدٍ وَّعَلٰٓى اٰلِ مُحَمَّدٍ كَمَا بَارَكْتَ عَلٰٓى اِبْرَاهِيْمَ وَعَلٰى اٰلِ اِبْرَاهِيْمَ ، اِنَّکَ حَمِيْدٌ مَّجِيْدٌ

Transliteration	Allah humma ṣalli 'alā Muḥammadin wa 'alā āli Muḥammadin kamā ṣallayta 'alā Ibraheema wa 'alā āli Ibraheema innaka ḥameedum majeed, Allah humma bārik 'alā Muḥammadin wa 'alā āli Muḥammadin kamā bārakta 'alā Ibraheema wa 'alā āli Ibraheema innaka ḥameedum majeed
Translation	O Allah! Let Your peace come upon Muhammad ﷺ and the family of Muhammad ﷺ as You have sent peace upon Ibrahim عليه السلام and the family of Ibrahim عليه السلام. Truly You are praiseworthy and glorious. O Allah! Bless Muhammad ﷺ and the family of Muhammad ﷺ as You have blessed Ibrahim عليه السلام and the family of Ibrahim عليه السلام. Truly You are praiseworthy and glorious

Du'ās After Ṣalāt 'Alan-Nabi (Durūd)

There are quite a lot of du'ās which Prophet ﷺ used to say after Durūd and he taught them to the Companions. Here we mention a few of them.

Abdullah bin Amr رضي الله عنه said that Abu Bakr رضي الله عنه said to the Messenger of Allah ﷺ, "Please teach me a du'ā so I can say it in my prayer." So, the Messenger of Allah ﷺ said:

Arabic	اَللّٰهُمَّ إِنِّي ظَلَمْتُ نَفْسِي ظُلْمًا كَثِيرًا وَلَا يَغْفِرُ الذُّنُوبَ إِلَّا أَنْتَ

	فَاغْفِرْلِي مَغْفِرَةً مِنْ عِنْدِكَ وَارْحَمْنِي إِنَّكَ أَنْتَ الْغَفُورُ الرَّحِيمُ
Transliteration	Allah humma innee ẓalamtu nafsee ẓulman katheeran wa la yaghfirudh dhunūba illa anta faghfirlee maghfiratam min ʻindika war ḥamnee innaka antal ghafūrur raḥeem
Translation	O Allah! I have been very cruel to myself (by ignoring my duty to You) and there is no one who can forgive the sins except You. So, forgive me because You are the only forgiver and have mercy on me. Verily, You are the forgiver and merciful. (Bukhari and Muslim)

Shadad bin Aus رضي الله عنه reported that the Prophet of Allah ﷺ used to say in his prayer:

Arabic	اَللَّهُمَّ إِنِّي أَسْأَلُكَ الثَّبَاتَ فِي الْأَمْرِ وَالْعَزِيمَةَ عَلَى الرُّشْدِ وَأَسْأَلُكَ شُكْرَ نِعْمَتِكَ وَحُسْنَ عِبَادَتِكَ وَأَسْأَلُكَ قَلْبًا سَلِيمًا وَلِسَانًا صَادِقًا وَأَسْأَلُكَ مِنْ خَيْرِ مَا تَعْلَمُ وَأَعُوذُ بِكَ مِنْ شَرِّ مَا تَعْلَمُ وَأَسْتَغْفِرُكَ لِمَا تَعْلَمُ
Transliteration	Allah humma innee as'alu kath thabāta fil amri wal ʻazeemata ʻalar rushdi wa as'aluka shukra niʻmatika wa ḥusna ʻibādatika wa as'aluka qalban saleeman

	wa lisānan sādiqan wa as'aluka min khayri mā ta'lamu, wa aūdhu bika min sharri ma ta'lamu wa astaghfiruka limā ta'lamu
Translation	O Allah! I ask You for strength in every matter of deen and strong willpower to be on the right path, and I ask You to make me thankful for Your bounties, and give me the ability to worship You perfectly, and I ask You to make my heart sincere and my tongue truthful. I ask You for every goodness known to You and I seek refuge in You from everything bad that You know is bad. I ask You forgiveness for all mistakes You know. (Nisai)

Aishah ؓ reported that the Prophet ﷺ used to say this du'ā in his prayers:

Arabic	اَللّٰهُمَّ إِنِّي أَعُوذُ بِكَ مِنْ عَذَابِ الْقَبْرِ وَأَعُوذُ بِكَ مِنْ فِتْنَةِ الْمَسِيحِ الدَّجَّالِ وَأَعُوذُ بِكَ مِنْ فِتْنَةِ الْمَحْيَا وَالْمَمَاتِ اَللّٰهُمَّ إِنِّي أَعُوذُ بِكَ مِنَ الْمَأْثَمِ وَالْمَغْرَمِ
Transliteration	Allah humma innee a'ūdhu bika min 'adhābil qabri wa a'ūdhu bika min fitna til maseeḥid dajjāli wa a'ūdhu bika min fitnatil maḥya wal mamāt Allah humma innee a'ūdhu bika minal ma'thami wal maghrami

Translation	O Allah! I seek refuge in You from the punishment of the grave, and I seek refuge in You from the troubles of Dajjal, and I seek refuge in You from the difficulties and troubles of life and death. O Allah! I seek refuge in You from every kind of sin and unexpected troubles. (Bukhari and Muslim)

Arabic	رَبِّ اجْعَلْنِي مُقِيمَ الصَّلَاةِ وَمِنْ ذُرِّيَّتِي رَبَّنَا وَتَقَبَّلْ دُعَاءِ رَبَّنَا اغْفِرْلِي وَلِوَالِدَيَّ وَلِلْمُؤْمِنِينَ يَوْمَ يَقُومُ الْحِسَابُ
Transliteration	Rabbij ʻalnee muqeemaṣ ṣalāti wa min dhurriyyatee, Rabbanā wa taqabbal duʻā, Rabba naghfirlee wali wālidayya wa lil mu'mineena yawma yaqumul ḥisāb
Translation	O Lord! Make me and my children keep up prayers, Our Lord, accept our prayer, Our Lord, forgive me and my parents and all the Believers on the Day of Judgement. (Surah Ibrahim 14:40-41)

Although most people read this duʻā after Durūd, it is permitted to recite any nice duʻā. However, it should be known that this duʻā is not one of those duʻās which Prophet ﷺ used to say after Durūd. It is preferable to read both Rabbij ʻalnee and the duʻās which are authentically proved from the Prophet ﷺ and those he taught to his Companions. We have mentioned only three but there are about twelve. However, they are too lengthy to mention here.

Ending the Prayer

After praying for himself as much as the person wishes, they should end the prayer saying:

Arabic	اَلسَلامُ عَلَيْكُم وَرَحْمَةُ اَللّٰهِ
Transliteration	As salāmu 'alaykum wa raḥmatullāh
Translation	Peace be on you and the mercy of Allah

turning the face first to the right and then to the left, both times over the shoulder. This brings the two, three or four rak'ahs of the prayer to completion.

Du'ās After Salutations

There are many du'ās which Prophet Muhammad ﷺ used to say after salutation. So, a person praying should try to memorise them and follow the practice of Prophet Muhammad ﷺ. Some of these du'ās we will mention here. It was the continuous practice of Prophet Muhammad ﷺ when he turned away from his prayer to say:

1. Immediately after Ṣalāḥ

Arabic	اَللّٰه أَكْبَر
Transliteration	Allāhu Akbar
Translation	Allah is the greatest

Arabic	أَسْتَغْفِرُ آللّٰه
Transliteration	Astaghfirullāh (3 times)
Translation	I ask Allah to forgive me

Arabic	اَللَّهُمَّ أَنْتَ السَّلاَمُ وَمِنْكَ السَّلاَمُ تَبَارَكْتَ يَا ذَا الْجَلاَلِ وَالإِكْرَامِ
Transliteration	Allah humma antas salāmu wa minkas salāmu, tabārakta yā dhul jalāli wal ikrām
Translation	O Allah! You are the peace and You are the source of peace You are blessed, O possessor of Glory and Honour. (Muslim)

2. Du'a of Gratitude to Allah

Arabic	اَللَّهُمَّ أَعِنِّيْ عَلَى ذِكْرِكَ وَشُكْرِكَ وَحُسْنِ عِبَادَتِكَ
Transliteration	Allah humma a'innee 'alā dhikrika wa shukrika wa ḥusni 'ibādatika
Translation	O Allah! Help me to remember You all the time and to thank You and worship You perfectly. (Ahmad and Abu Dawud)

3. Du'a of Great Praise of Allah

Arabic	لاَ إِلَهَ إِلَّا اللهُ وَحْدَهُ لاَ شَرِيكَ لَهُ لَهُ الْمُلْكُ وَلَهُ الْحَمْدُ وَهُوَ عَلَى كُلِّ شَيْءٍ قَدِيرٌ اَللَّهُمَّ لاَ مَانِعَ لِمَا أَعْطَيْتَ وَلاَ مُعْطِيَ لِمَا مَنَعْتَ وَلاَ يَنْفَعُ ذَا الْجَدِّ مِنْكَ الْجَدُّ

Transliteration	Lā ilāha illallāhu waḥdahū lā shareeka lahū lahul mulku wala hul ḥamdu wa huwa 'ala kulli shay'in qadeer, Allahumma lā māni'a limā a'ṭayta wa lā mu'ṭiya limā mana'ta wa lā yanfa'u dhal jaddi minkal jadd
Translation	There is no God but Allah, He is the only One and has no partner, Sovereignty and praise are only for Him, and He has full authority over everything. O Allah! None can prevent what You have willed to bestow and none can bestow what You have willed to prevent, and no wealth or majesty can benefit anyone, as from You is all wealth and majesty. (Bukhari and Muslim)

4. It is Sunnah to Say:

Arabic	سُبْحَانَ ٱللهِ ٱلْحَمْدُ لِلَّهِ اَللّٰهُ أَكْبَرُ
Transliteration	SubhānAllāh (33 times) Alhamdulillāh (33 times) Allāhu Akbar (34 times)
Translation	Glory be to Allah Praise be to Allah Allah is the greatest

There are very many du'ās which the Prophet ﷺ used to say and he taught them to his Companions. These can be found in the famous books of hadiths.

Praying in Congregation

When praying fard in congregation, the Imam should recite Sūrah Fātiḥah and any sūrah or part of the Qur'an aloud in the Fajr prayer, first two rak'ahs of the Maghrib prayer and the first two rak'ahs of the 'Isha prayer. This means that the Imam will recite in silence in the Ẓuhr and 'Asr prayers.

Congregational prayer is almost obligatory in fard prayer but there are some occasional optional prayers which are preferable to offer in congregation; for example, 'Eid prayer, Tarāweeh prayer, Rain prayer etc. However, it is preferable to pray the usual nafl prayer alone. Every prayer must be started with takbeer taḥrimah and finished with a salutation.

CHAPTER 5: SAJDAH AS-SAHW (SAJDAH FOR FORGETFULNESS)

If a person makes a mistake during his prayer, what should they do? Sajdah as-Sahw is allowed when:

(i) A person praying becomes confused or forgets the number of rak'ahs performed.
(ii) They get up after the second rak'ah when they should have remained in the sitting position and recited tashahhud.

In either of these cases, the person has to base the prayer on the certainty of their memory and do two sajdahs (sajdah as-sahw) before the salutation. In other words, sajdah as-sahw compensates the shortcoming in the prayer.

Evidence
Abdullah bin Bujainah رضي الله عنه narrated that the Messenger of Allah ﷺ led them in the Ẓuhr prayer. He stood up after the first two rak'ahs and did not sit for tashahhud; so the people stood up with him as well. When he had completed the prayer and the people were waiting for his salutation, he said Allāhu Akbar while he was sitting and did two sajdahs before the salutation. Then he said the salutation. (Bukhari and Muslim)
Abu Sa'id al Khudri رضي الله عنه narrated that the Messenger of Allah ﷺ said: "When one of you becomes confused during his prayer and he does not know how many rak'ahs he has offered (three or four), he should ignore what is doubtful and base his prayer on what he believes is certain. Then he should do two extra sajdahs before the salutation. If he had prayed five rak'ahs, then these two sajdahs will make his prayer six rak'ahs (two of which will be nafl), and if he had prayed the correct number of rak'ahs then these two sajdahs will be humility for the devil." (Muslim)

These hadiths prove that sajdah as-sahw should be done before the salutation but there are hadiths which prove that the Prophet ﷺ did two sajdahs (sajdah as-sahw) after the salutation.

Evidence
Abdullah bin Jafar ؓ narrated from the Prophet ﷺ that he said: "Anyone who has become confused and doubtful in his prayer, he should do two extra sajdahs after he has given the salutation." (Ahmad, Abu Dawud, Nisai and Ibn Khuzaimah)

There is no contradiction between these hadiths. Both ways are proved by the Prophet ﷺ; it is up to the believer to choose one. They both can be practised but it seems that the first method, that is, doing two sajdahs just before the salutation, is more reasonable, more authentic and more widely practiced by the muḥadditheen and 'ulamā.

WHEN SHOULD A PERSON DO SAJDAH AS-SAHW

1. If one is doubtful about the number of rak'ahs they have prayed.

2. If one forgets to sit in the first tashahhud and gets up for the third rak'ah.

3. If one finishes the prayer forgetfully without completing the number of rak'ahs one intended to pray.

Note: Sajdah as-sahw is not sufficient replacement for missing the actions of the prayer which are considered as rukn (obligatory elements) of the prayer. These are: niyyah, takbeer taḥrimah, qiyam (standing position between takbeer taḥrimah and rukū'), rukū', and both sajdahs.

CHAPTER 6: OCCASIONAL PRAYERS

WITR PRAYER

Witr prayer is sunnat mu'akkadah. It is very much emphasised by Prophet Muhammad ﷺ. He did not leave this prayer even during a journey or when mounted on camelback. It was emphasised to the extent that some Muslim scholars understood it to be wajib (compulsory) but after a careful study of hadiths, it can be said that it is not wajib but a very much emphasised prayer.

Witr prayer is often mistakenly thought of as part of the 'Isha prayer. This is not so. Witr prayer is a separate prayer which can be offered after the 'Isha prayer right up to the break of dawn. For the convenience of the believers, the Prophet ﷺ allowed Witr to be offered straight after 'Isha.

In Arabic, the word witr means 'one'. In a hadith, the Messenger of Allah ﷺ says: "Allah is one, so he likes the number one." (Muslim) Allah also likes odd numbers because when an odd number is divided by two, the remainder is always one. For this reason, the Prophet ﷺ preferred odd numbers. He liked to do things in odd numbers in his routine life also, such as, saying prayers, reciting du'ās, eating dates etc. That is why Prophet ﷺ asked the believers to pray Witr at the end of the night prayer so that it can make the night prayer into an odd number.

Evidence
Abdullah bin Umar ؓ says that the Messenger of Allah ﷺ said: "Night prayer is to be offered in two rak'ah units. When one of you feels that dawn is near then he should offer one rak'ah which can make all the night prayer he offered into an odd number." (Bukhari and Muslim)

Number of Rak'ahs of Witr Prayer

Evidence
Abdullah bin Umar رضي الله عنه said that the Messenger of Allah ﷺ said: "Witr prayer is one rak'ah at the end of the nafl prayer at night."
Abu Ayub رضي الله عنه says that Prophet Muhammad ﷺ said: "Every Muslim should pray Witr. Anyone who likes to pray five rak'ahs of Witr he should do so, anyone who likes to pray three rak'ahs, he should do so, and anyone who likes to pray one rak'ah, he should do so." (Abu Dawud, Nisai and Ibn Majah)

We understand from the above mentioned hadith that the actual Witr prayer is one rak'ah, although a person can offer 1, 3, 5, 7 or 9 rak'ahs of Witr prayer. All of these numbers are approved by Prophet Muhammad ﷺ in authentic hadiths.

Time of Witr Prayer

Witr prayer can be offered after the 'Isha prayer right up to the break of dawn.

Evidence
Aishah رضي الله عنها said: "Prophet Muhammad ﷺ prayed Witr during all times of the night. Sometimes he prayed Witr during the first part of the night, sometimes during the middle part of the night, and sometimes during the end part of the night but he used to complete the prayer before the break of dawn." (Bukhari and Muslim)

However, a person who thinks they will not get up to pray Witr at the end part of the night can offer Witr immediately after 'Isha or before they go to bed. But someone who thinks that they can get up and pray nafl at night should pray Witr at the end of their night prayer.

Evidence
Jabir ﷺ said that the Prophet ﷺ said: "Anyone of you who cannot get up at the end part of the night, he should pray Witr in the first part of the night and anyone of you who thinks he can get up at the end part of the night, he should pray Witr then, because the angels are present for the prayer offered at the end part of the night." (Muslim, Ahmad, Tirmidhi and Ibn Majah)

How to Pray Witr

When praying one Witr, a person can offer it as the usual prayer.

When praying 3, 5, 7 or 9 rak'ahs of Witr, prayer there is more than one way the prayer can be offered. For example:

a) A person praying three rak'ahs Witr can pray two rak'ahs like the usual prayer. After the salutation of As salāmu 'alaykum wa raḥmatullāh, first to the right and then to the left, they should get up immediately to complete the third rak'ah. This way of offering Witr prayer is called Witr bil fasal.
b) A person praying three rak'ahs or five rak'ahs Witr should not sit for tashahhud in between the rak'ahs except in the last rak'ah.
c) A person praying three, five or seven rak'ahs Witr should sit in tashahhud in the last but one rak'ah, e.g. in the second rak'ah if they are offering three Witr, fourth rak'ah if they are offering five Witr, or sixth rak'ah if they are offering seven Witr and so on. They should read tashahhud and then get up for the last rak'ah and complete it.

All three methods are authentic and are practised by the great 'ulamā.

Evidence
The Prophet ﷺ said: "Do not make your Witr prayer similar to your Maghrib prayer." (Qiyamul-Layl of Muhammad bin Nasar al Marwazi)

Du'ā Qunūt in Witr Prayer

Reading du'ā qunūt in the last rak'ah of the Witr Prayer is a proven practice of Prophet Muhammad ﷺ and it can be read before rukū' or after rukū'.

Evidence
Humaid ؓ narrated that he asked Anas ؓ about the du'ā qunūt whether it should be read before the rukū' or after the rukū'. Anas ؓ replied, "We used to say it before the rukū' and after the rukū'." (Ibn Majah, Qiyamul-Layl of Muhammad bin Nasar al Marwazi and Fathul Bari)

Although du'ā qunūt can be said before the rukū', it is more authentic and more approved to say it after the rukū'.

a) Someone who wants to read du'ā qunūt before rukū' should read it after they have finished reciting Sūrah Fātiḥah and a chapter of the Holy Qur'an. While reciting du'ā qunūt a person can cup their hands in front or leave them folded.
b) Someone who wants to read du'ā qunūt after the rukū' should read it with their hands cupped in front or they can let their hands rest at the sides. Saying du'ā qunūt after the rukū' and cupping the hands in front is preferable as this was the practice of Prophet Muhammad ﷺ.

Note: Some fuqahā insist that reading du'ā qunūt is compulsory in the last rak'ah of the Witr and some others say it is compulsory in the last rak'ah of the Fajr prayer, but if you study hadiths carefully you will find that it is not compulsory either in the Witr or in the Fajr prayer. Therefore, if a person leaves du'ā qunūt in the Witr prayer, their prayer will not be deficient. Also if someone does not know du'ā qunūt, they need not say another sūrah of the Qur'an or any other words in its place. Du'ā qunūt can be read in any prayer.

Text of Du'a Qunūt

Hasan bin Āli رضي الله عنه said the, "Messenger of Allah ﷺ taught me the words which I should say in the du'ā of Witr and those are as follows:

Arabic	اَللّٰهُمَّ اهْدِنِىْ فِيْمَنْ هَدَيْتَ وَعَافِنِى فِيْمَنْ عَافَيْتَ وَتَوَلَّنِىْ فِيْمَنْ تَوَلَّيْتَ وَبَارِكْ لِىْ فِيْمَا اَعْطَيْتَ وَقِنِيْ شَرَّ مَا قَضَيْتَ فَاِنَّكَ تَقْضِىْ وَلَا يُقْضَى عَلَيْكَ وَاِنَّهُ لَا يَذِلُّ مَنْ وَّالَيْتَ وَلَا يَعِزُّ مَنْ عَادَيْتَ تَبَارَكْتَ رَبَّنَا وَتَعَالَيْتَ فَلَكَ الْحَمْدُ عَلٰى مَا قَضَيْتَ وَاَسْتَغْفِرُكَ وَاَتُوْبُ اِلَيْكَ وَصَلَّى اللّٰهُ عَلٰى سَيِّدِنَا مُحَمَّدٍ النَّبِيِّ الْاُمِّيِّ وَعَلٰى آلِهٖ وَصَحْبِهٖ وَسَلَّمَ
Transliteration	Allah hum mahdinee feeman hadayta wa 'āfinee feeman 'āfayta wa tawallanee feeman tawallayta wa barik lee feema a'ṭayta wa qinee sharra ma qaḍayta fa innaka taqḍee wala yuqḍa 'alayka wa innahū lā yadhillu man wālayta wa lā ya'izzu man 'ādayta tabarakta rabbanā wa ta'ālayta fa lakal ḥamdu 'ala mā qaḍayta wa astaghfiruka wa atūbu ilayka wa ṣallallāhu 'alā sayyidinā Muḥammadin nabee yil ummee wa 'alā ālihee wa ṣaḥbihee wa sallam. (Abu Dawud, Nisai and Ibn Majah)

Translation	O Allah, make me among those whom You have guided, and make me among those whom You have saved, and make me among those whom You have chosen, and bless whatever You have given me, and protect me from the evil which You have decreed; verily, You decide the things and nobody can decide against You; and surely the person You befriend cannot be disgraced, and the person You oppose cannot be honoured. You are blessed, our Lord, and exalted, so to You is all praise for what You have decreed. I ask You Your forgiveness and turn to You. And the blessings of Allah be upon our master Muhammad, the unlettered Prophet, and his family and Companions and grant them the best of peace. (Abu Dawud, Nisai, Ibn Majah and Tirmidhi)

Arabic	اَللّٰهُمَّ إِنا نَسْتَعِينُكَ وَنَسْتَغْفِرُكَ وَنُؤْمِنُ بِكَ وَنَتَوَكَّلُ عَلَيْكَ وَنُثْنِىْ عَلَيْكَ الخَيْرَ وَنَشْكُرُكَ وَلَا نَكْفُرُكَ وَنَخْلَعُ وَنَتْرُكُ مَنْ يَّفْجُرُكَ اَللّٰهُمَّ إِيَّاكَ نَعْبُدُ وَلَكَ نُصَلِّىْ وَنَسْجُدُ وَإِلَيْكَ نَسْعٰى وَنَحْفِدُ وَنَرْجُو رَحْمَتَكَ وَنَخْشٰى عَذَابَكَ إِنَّ عَذَابَكَ بِالكُفَّارِ مُلْحَقٌ

Transliteration	Allah humma innā nasta'eenuka wa nastaghfiruka wa nu'minu bika wa natawakkalu 'alayka wa nuthnee 'alaykal khayra wa nashkuruka wa lā nakfuruka wa nakhla'u wa natruku man yafjuruka, Allah humma iyyāka na'budu wa laka nuṣallee wa nasjudu wa ilayka nas'ā wa naḥfidu wa narjū raḥmataka wa nakhshā 'adhābaka inna 'adhābaka bil kuffāri mulḥiq
Translation	O Allah! We ask You for help and seek Your forgiveness, and we believe in You and have trust in You, and we praise You in the best way and we thank You and we are not ungrateful to You, and we forsake and turn away from the one who disobeys You. O Allah! We worship You only and pray to You and prostrate ourselves before You, and we run towards You and serve You, and we hope to receive Your mercy, and we fear Your punishment. Surely, the disbelievers will receive Your punishment

Some 'ulamā recommend this du'ā in the Witr prayer. Of course, it can be read as it is a nice du'ā but it is not one of those du'ās which Prophet Muhammad ﷺ read in his Witr prayer. There are some other du'ās which Prophet Muhammad ﷺ read in his qunūt in the Witr prayer or in his other prayers.

A person can read all these du'ās together or just one of them or combine them with other du'ās.

JUMU'AH (FRIDAY PRAYER)

Importance of Attending Friday Prayer

Friday Prayer is very important in Islam. It has its own moral, social and political benefits and is obligatory for every Muslim except women, children, seriously ill people and travellers. They can pray Jumu'ah but it is not obligatory on them.

Prophet Muhammad ﷺ has given a strong warning to the person who leaves his Jumu'ah prayer without a good reason.

Evidence
Abdullah bin Masud ؓ narrated that the Messenger of Allah ﷺ once said about the people who did not come to the Friday Prayer without a good reason: "I wish to appoint someone to lead the prayer and myself go to the houses of those who missed the Friday Prayer and set fire to their houses with the occupants in them." (Muslim and Ahmad)
"A person who leaves three Friday prayers consecutively, Allah puts a seal on his heart." (Ahmad, Tirmidhi and Abu Dawud)

Importance of Cleanliness for Friday Prayer

Because in Friday Prayer a comparatively large number of Muslims gather in a big place, so Islam emphasises on the physical cleanliness of the worshippers as well.

Evidence
The Prophet ﷺ said: "A person who has a bath on Friday, cleanses himself fully, uses oil and perfume; then goes to the mosque early in the afternoon and takes his place quietly without pushing or disturbing people; then he prays (optional prayer as much as he was able to pray); then sits quietly listening to the Khutbah, he will be forgiven his sins between this Jumu'ah and the next Jumu'ah." (Bukhari)

Importance of Going Early to Friday Prayer

On Friday, it is more rewarding to get ready quickly to go to the mosque.

Evidence
Abu Hurairah ؓ narrated that the Messenger of Allah ﷺ said: "On Friday the angels stand at the door of the mosque and write down the

names of the people in the order in which they enter the mosque for Friday prayer. The first group of people who enter the mosque get the reward equivalent to that of sacrificing a camel, the people who enter the mosque after them get the reward equivalent to that of sacrificing a cow. The people who enter the mosque after them get the reward equivalent to that of sacrificing a ram and the people who follow on likewise get this reward of a chicken, egg and so on. There is a gradation of rewards for the people as they enter. The angels keep writing the names of the people as they enter the mosque until the Imam sits down to give the Khutbah. Then the angels collect their registers and sit and listen to the Khutbah." (Bukhari and Muslim)

Prayer Before Jumu'ah

A person who goes to attend Friday prayer can pray as many nafl as he wishes after the sun has declined from its zenith to when the imam comes to give the Khutbah. Anyhow he is expected to pray at least two rak'ahs sunnah.

Listening to the Khutbah (Sermon)

Once the Khutbah starts, the whole congregation should listen to it in silence. If a person arrives while the imam is giving Khutbah, then this person should pray two rak'ahs nafl before sitting down to listen to the Khutbah.

Evidence
Jabir ﵁ said that the Messenger of Allah ﷺ said while he was giving Khutbah: "If anyone of you goes to attend the Friday Prayer while the Imam is delivering Khutbah he should pray two rak'ahs and should not make them long." (Muslim)
Jabir ﵁ says that once a man came to Friday Prayer while the Messenger of Allah ﷺ was delivering Khutbah, so Allah's Messenger ﷺ asked him, "Did you pray?" "No," he answered. Then Prophet ﷺ

said to him, "Stand up and pray." (Bukhari, Muslim, Abu Dawud and Tirmidhi)
Abu Qatadah ؓ says that the Messenger of Allah ﷺ said: "Whenever one of you enters the mosque he should not sit down without offering two rak'ahs." (Bukhari and Muslim)

It is a continuous practice in some mosques that those who arrive while the Imam is giving his Khutbah, sit down and listen to it. When the Imam has finished his Khutbah, he gives time to the late arrivals to pray two or four rak'ahs sunnah. After that the imam gives a short Khutbah in Arabic before praying the Jumu'ah Prayer.

Some members of the congregation feel that it is disrespectful to the Imam if someone offers two rak'ahs sunnah while the he is delivering the Khutbah. This is incorrect and unproven from the practice of Prophet Muhammad ﷺ, as the hadiths above prove.

Actual Jumu'ah Prayer

Jumu'ah Prayer is two rak'ahs fard. If a person is late and finds only one rak'ah with the congregation, he should complete the second rak'ah alone. If a person arrives so late that he misses the Jumu'ah prayer completely, then he has to offer four rak'ahs fard of Ẓuhr prayer. The Jumu'ah Prayer is the replacement of Ẓuhr prayer but the Imam should do the recitation (qir'at) aloud in the Jumu'ah Prayer.

Prayer After Jumu'ah

After the Jumu'ah Prayer, two rak'ahs of sunnah prayer is an authentically proven practice of Prophet Muhammad ﷺ but some Companions used to pray four or six rak'ahs sunnah after the Jumu'ah Prayer.

Evidence
Ibn Umar ؓ said that the Messenger of Allah ﷺ did not pray after the Friday Prayer until he went home and then he prayed two rak'ahs. (Bukhari and Muslim)

Evidence
Abu Hurairah ﷺ narrated that the Messenger of Allah ﷺ said: "Any one of you who is going to pray after the Friday Prayer, he should pray four rak'ahs." (Muslim)
Ata says: "Whenever Abdullah bin Umar ﷺ prayed Jumu'ah in Makkah, he would move a little forward after the Jumu'ah prayer and offer two rak'ahs; then he would move a little forward again and offer four rak'ahs. And whenever he prayed Jumu'ah in Madinah, he did not pray in the Mosque after the Jumu'ah Prayer until he went back home. Then he prayed two rak'ahs. When he was asked why he did not pray in the mosque after the Jumu'ah prayer, he answered, 'This was the practice of Prophet Muhammad ﷺ.'"

These hadiths clarify that two, four or six rak'ahs can be offered after the Jumu'ah Prayer according to the time and capacity of the person. It is not good practice to accuse people who read two rak'ahs only because this, too, was the authentic practice of Prophet Muhammad ﷺ.

'EID PRAYER

Place for 'Eid Prayer

'Eid Prayer should be offered outdoor in the open, e.g. in a park, field, or a desert etc. If it is wet or not possible to find a suitable outdoor place it can be prayed in a mosque or a large hall. (Abu Dawud)

Time of 'Eid Prayer

'Eid Prayer should be offered when the sun can be seen clearly above the horizon.

Number of Rak'ahs of 'Eid Prayer

'Eid Prayer is two rak'ahs. There is no nafl prayer before or after the 'Eid Prayer. There is no iqāmah or adhān for 'Eid Prayer.

Evidence
Ibn Abbas ﵁ reported: "No doubt, Prophet Muhammad ﷺ used to pray two rak'ahs only for 'Eid Prayer. He did not pray anything before or afterwards." (Bukhari and Muslim)

Conduct of 'Eid Prayer

The two rak'ahs of 'Eid Prayer should be offered in the same manner as the two rak'ahs of the usual prayer except that there are seven takbeers in the first rak'ah and five takbeers in the second rak'ah. With each extra takbeer, the hands should be raised up to the shoulder level (as in takbeer taḥrimah). All extra takbeers should be pronounced before starting qir'at (recitation).

Evidence
Kathir bin Abdullah reported from his father and his father from his grandfather that the Prophet ﷺ said seven takbeers in the first rak'ah of 'Eid Prayer and five takbeers in the second rak'ah of 'Eid Prayer before beginning recitation. (Tirmidhi, Ibn Majah and Darimi)

'Eid Prayer is Offered Before Khutbah

Evidence
Jafar bin Muhammad ﵁ reported: "No doubt, Prophet Muhammad ﷺ, Abu Bakr ﵁ and Umar ﵁ said seven extra takbeers in the first rak'ah of their 'Eid and Rain Prayers and five extra takbeers in the second rak'ah of their 'Eid and Rain Prayers. The Prophet ﷺ offered 'Eid Prayer before Khutbah and recited aloud." (Shafa'i)

RAIN PRAYER

The Rain Prayer is a special prayer which is offered during a period of drought. Muslims are asked to pray two rak'ahs nafl out in the open and make a special du'ā for rain.

JANĀZAH PRAYER (FUNERAL PRAYER)

It is a right of a Muslim that when someone passes away, other Muslims should pray Janāzah Prayer for them. Janāzah Prayer is a supererogatory prayer. If no one from the whole of the Muslim community prays the Janāzah Prayer, then the whole community will be considered sinful in the sight of Allah. If some of the people pray the Janāzah Prayer, then the whole community is saved from the anger of Allah ﷻ even though the reward will only be given to the participants.

In hadiths, Prophet Muhammad ﷺ emphasised and encouraged the Muslims to attend funeral ceremonies. So, every Muslim male should try his best to fulfil his duty for the deceased.

1. Janāzah Prayer should be prayed in congregation as this is more rewarding. It can be prayed in more than one congregation but by different people.
2. Janāzah Prayer should be offered in an open place but in case of rain or bad weather or any other reason it can be prayed in a mosque or a hall etc.

While Praying Janāzah Prayer

If the body is that of a male, the Imam should stand level with the head and shoulders of the dead body, while for a female, the Imam should stand level with the middle part of the body.

Where Janāzah Prayer Differs

Janāzah Prayer is only slightly different from other prayers in that there is no rukū', no sajdah, and no tashahhud in it. There is no fixed time for offering this prayer. It has to be prayed in a standing position only. The other conditions such as purification, facing Qiblah, sutrah, dress etc. have to be satisfied as in the usual prayers.

Conduct of the Janāzah Prayer

a) Like other prayers facing Qiblah is a necessary condition. The Imam should ask the people to straighten their rows. There should be an odd number of rows as it is more rewarding.
b) Making intention is necessary in Janāzah Prayer as it is necessary in other prayers. Before beginning prayer the intention should be made in the heart as uttering any words of niyah aloud was not the practice of Prophet Muhammad ﷺ or of his Companions.

First Takbeer or Takbeer Taḥrimah

Janāzah Prayer contains four takbeers. The first takbeer is takbeer taḥrimah. The Imam says Allāhu Akbar and raises his hands up to shoulder level with fingers stretching to the earlobes and the congregation does the same. Then the Imam folds his hands on his chest, right hand over left.

Du'ā of Starting

Then the person can read one of those du'ās which are recommended in the first rak'ah of the usual prayer before recitation of Sūrah Fātiḥah. For example:

Arabic	سُبْحَانَكَ اللَّهُمَّ وَبِحَمْدِكَ وَتَبَارَكَ اسْمُكَ وَتَعَالَى جَدُّكَ وَلاَ إِلَهَ غَيْرُكَ
Transliteration	Subhāna kallah humma wabi ḥamdika watabāra kasmuka wata 'āla jadduka wa lā ilāha ghayruka
Translation	Glory be to You, O Allah, and all praises are due unto You and blessed is Your name and high is Your majesty and none is worthy of worship but You

Or he can say other du'ās. Some scholars do not recommend du'ā of starting in Janāzah prayer but reading it is preferable. However, if someone does not read it, it does not affect their prayer. Both ways are practised by Muslim scholars.

Then the person should say:

Arabic	أَعُوذُ بِاللهِ مِنَ الشَّيْطَانِ الرَّجِيمِ
Transliteration	A'ūdhu billāhi minash shayṭā nir rajeem
Translation	I seek Allah's protection from satan who is accursed

Arabic	بِسْمِ ٱللَّهِ ٱلرَّحْمَٰنِ ٱلرَّحِيمِ
Transliteration	Bismillāh hir raḥmān nir raḥeem
Translation	In the name of Allah, the Most Gracious and the Most Merciful

Arabic	اَلْحَمْدُ لِلَّهِ رَبِّ الْعَالَمِينَ اَلرَّحْمَنِ الرَّحِيمِ مَالِكِ يَوْمِ الدِّينِ إِيَّاكَ نَعْبُدُ وَإِيَّاكَ نَسْتَعِينُ إِهْدِنَا الصِّرَاطَ الْمُسْتَقِيمَ صِرَاطَ الَّذِينَ أَنْعَمْتَ عَلَيْهِمْ غَيْرِ الْمَغْضُوبِ عَلَيْهِمْ وَلَا الضَّالِّينَ
Transliteration	Alḥamdu lillāhi rabbil 'ālameen, Ar raḥmān nir raḥeem, Māliki yawmid deen, Iyyāka na'budu wa iyyāka nasta'een, Ihdinas ṣirāṭal mustaqeem, Ṣirāṭal ladheena an'amta 'alayhim,

	Ghayril maghḍūbi 'alayhim walad ḍālleen, (Āmeen)
Translation	Praise is only for Allah, Lord of the Universe, The Most Kind, the Most Merciful, The Master of the Day of Judgement, You alone we worship and to You alone we pray for help, Show us the Straight Way, the way of those whom You have blessed, who have not deserved Your anger nor gone astray. (Ameen)

Some people do not read Sūrah Fātiḥah in Janāzah Prayer but Sūrah Fātiḥah is necessary for the validity of any type of prayer as Prophet Muhammad ﷺ has said that no prayer is valid without Sūrah Fātiḥah.

Evidence
Talha bin Abdullah bin Auf رضي الله عنه said that he prayed behind Abdullah bin Abbas رضي الله عنه and Abdullah bin Abbas رضي الله عنه read Sūrah Fātiḥah aloud. Afterwards he said, "I read it out loud so that you may know that it is the sunnah of Prophet Muhammad ﷺ." (Bukhari)

This hadith proves that reciting Sūrah Fātiḥah is necessary in Janāzah Prayer as well.

Recitation of a Sūrah

A sūrah or part of a sūrah can be read after the recitation of Sūrah Fātiḥah but it is not essential to read it.

Second Takbeer

Then the imam should say the second takbeer and the congregation should follow but it is not necessary to raise the hands up to the shoulder level but if someone does, it is alright. Both ways are practiced by great 'ulamā.

After the second takbeer, the person praying Janāzah Prayer should recite Durūd in his heart. It is preferable to read the Durūd which a person reads in tashahhud of his usual prayer as follows:

Arabic	اَللّٰهُمَّ صَلِّ عَلٰى مُحَمَّدٍ وَّعَلٰٓى اٰلِ مُحَمَّدٍ کَمَا صَلَّيْتَ عَلٰٓى اِبْرَاهِيْمَ وَعَلٰٓى اٰلِ اِبْرَاهِيْمَ اِنَّکَ حَمِيْدٌ مَّجِيْدٌ اَللّٰهُمَّ بَارِکْ عَلٰى مُحَمَّدٍ وَّعَلٰٓى اٰلِ مُحَمَّدٍ کَمَا بَارَکْتَ عَلٰٓى اِبْرَاهِيْمَ وَعَلٰٓى اٰلِ اِبْرَاهِيْمَ اِنَّکَ حَمِيْدٌ مَّجِيْدٌ
Transliteration	Allah humma ṣalli ‘alā Muḥammadin wa ‘alā āli Muḥammadin kamā ṣallayta ‘alā Ibraheema wa ‘alā āli Ibraheema innaka ḥameedum majeed, Allah humma bārik ‘alā Muḥammadin wa ‘alā āli Muḥammadin kamā bārakta ‘alā Ibraheema wa ‘alā āli Ibraheema innaka ḥameedum majeed
Translation	O Allah! Let Your peace come upon Muhammad ﷺ and the family of Muhammad ﷺ as You have sent peace upon Ibrahim عَلَيْهِ السَّلَام and the family of Ibrahim عَلَيْهِ السَّلَام, Truly You are praiseworthy and glorious, O Allah! Bless Muhammad ﷺ and the family of Muhammad ﷺ

	as You have blessed Ibrahim عليه السلام and the family of Ibrahim عليه السلام, Truly You are praiseworthy and glorious

Third Takbeer

Then the imam should say the third takbeer and the congregation should follow in which each person should pray for the deceased. Alternatively, the imam can pray out loud and the congregation can say āmeen after him. All kinds of du'ās for the benefit of the deceased can be said.

Abu Hurairah رضي الله عنه said that the Messenger of Allah ﷺ prayed Janāzah of a Muslim and he said in his du'ā:

Arabic	اَللَّهُمَّ اغْفِرْ لِحَيِّنَا وَمَيِّتِنَا وَشَاهِدِنَا وَغَائِبِنَا وَصَغِيرِنَا وَكَبِيرِنَا وَذَكَرِنَا وَأُنْثَانَا اَللَّهُمَّ مَنْ أَحْيَيْتَهُ مِنَّا فَأَحْيِهِ عَلَى الإِسْلَامِ وَمَنْ تَوَفَّيْتَهُ مِنَّا فَتَوَفَّهُ عَلَى الإِيمَانِ، اَللَّهُمَّ لَا تَحْرِمْنَا أَجْرَهُ وَلَا تُضِلَّنَا بَعْدَهُ
Transliteration	Allahumm aghfir li ḥayyinā wa mayyitinā wa shāhidinā wa ghā'ibinā wa ṣagheerinā wa kabeerinā wa dhakarinā wa unthānā, Allahumma man aḥyaytahū minnā fa aḥyihee 'alal Islāmi wa man tawaffaytahu minnā fa tawaffahu 'alal eemaani, Allahumma lā taḥrimnā ajrahū wa lā tuḍillanā ba'dah
Translation	O Allah! Forgive our people who are still alive and who have passed away, Forgive those who are present here and those who are absent, Forgive our young and our elderly, Forgive our males and our females

	O Allah! The one whom You wish to keep alive from among us, let him remain alive on Islam and the one You wish to die, let him in die in faith. Oh Allah! Do not deprive us from his reward and do not put us in hardship or any type of trial after his death. (Ahmad, Abu Dawud, Tirmidhi and Ibn Majah)

Auf bin Malik ؓ said that that the Messenger of Allah ﷺ prayed a Janāzah Prayer and I heard him saying the following du'ā and I memorised it:

Arabic	اَللّٰهُمَّ اغْفِرْ لَهُ وَارْحَمْهُ وَعَافِهِ وَاعْفُ عَنْهُ وَأَكْرِمْ نُزُلَهُ وَوَسِّعْ مُدْخَلَهُ وَاغْسِلْهُ بِالْمَاءِ وَالثَّلْجِ وَالْبَرَدِ وَنَقِّهِ مِنَ الْخَطَايَا كَمَا نَقَّيْتَ الثَّوْبَ الْأَبْيَضَ مِنَ الدَّنَسِ وَأَبْدِلْهُ دَارًا خَيْرًا مِنْ دَارِهِ وَأَهْلًا خَيْرًا مِنْ أَهْلِهِ وَزَوْجًا خَيْرًا مِنْ زَوْجِهِ وَأَدْخِلْهُ الْجَنَّةَ وَأَعِذْهُ مِنْ عَذَابِ الْقَبْرِ وَعَذَابِ النَّارِ
Transliteration	Allah hum maghfir lahū war ḥamhū wa 'afihee wa'fu 'anhū wa akrim nuzuluhū wa was si' mudkhalahū waghsilhū bil ma'i wath thalji wal baradi, wa naqqihi minal khaṭāyā kamā naqqaytath thawbal abyaḍa minad danasi, wa abdilhū dāran khayram min dārihi wa ahlan khayram min ahlihee wa zawjan khayram min zawjihee wa adkhil hul jannata, wa a'idh hū min 'adhābil qabri wa 'adhāban nār

Translation	O Allah, forgive him, have mercy on him, pardon him, grant him security, provide him a nice place and spacious lodgings, wash him (off from his sins) with water, snow and ice, purify him from his sins as a white garment is cleansed from dirt, replace his present abode with a better one, replace his present family with a better one, replace his present partner with a better one, make him enter paradise and see him from the trials of grave and the punishment of hell. (Muslim)

For a female:

Arabic	اَللّٰهُمَّ اغْفِرْ لَهَا وَارْحَمْهَا وَعَافِهَا وَاعْفُ عَنْهَا وَأَكْرِمْ نُزُلَهَا وَوَسِّعْ مُدْخَلَهَا وَاغْسِلْهَا بِالْمَاءِ وَالثَّلْجِ وَالْبَرَدِ وَنَقِّهَا مِنَ الْخَطَايَا كَمَا نَقَّيْتَ الثَّوْبَ الْأَبْيَضَ مِنَ الدَّنَسِ وَأَبْدِلْهَا دَارًا خَيْرًا مِنْ دَارِهَا وَأَهْلًا خَيْرًا مِنْ أَهْلِهَا وَزَوْجًا خَيْرًا مِنْ زَوْجِهَا وَأَدْخِلْهَا الْجَنَّةَ وَأَعِذْهَا مِنْ عَذَابِ الْقَبْرِ وَعَذَابِ النَّارِ
Transliteration	Allah hum maghfir lahā war ḥamhā wa ‘afihā wa‘fu ‘anhā wa akrim nuzuluhā wa was si‘ mudkhalahā waghsilhā bil ma’i wath thalji wal baradi, wa naqqihā minal khaṭāyā kamā naqqaytath thawbal abyaḍu minad danasi, wa abdilhā dāran khayram min dārihā wa ahlan khayram min ahlihā wa zawjan khayram min

	zawjihā wa adkhil hal jannata, wa a'idh hā min 'adhābil qabri wa 'adhāban nār
Translation	O Allah! Forgive her, have mercy on her, pardon her, grant her security, provide her a nice place and spacious lodgings, wash her (off from her sins) with water, snow and ice; purify her from her sins as a white garment is cleansed from dirt, replace her present abode with a better one, replace her present family with a better one, replace her present partner with a better one, make her enter paradise and see her from the trials of grave and the punishment of hell

One thing we can see clearly from the above mentioned hadiths is that every Companion who narrated the du'ā of Janāzah Prayer says that he had heard the Prophet ﷺ saying the words of du'ā in Janāzah Prayer. This proves that the Messenger of Allah ﷺ used to say the Janāzah Prayer or at least the du'ās in Janāzah Prayer aloud. Therefore, there should not be any objection or confusion if the Imam recites aloud in Janāzah Prayer.

There are some other du'ās which are narrated from Prophet Muhammad ﷺ and they can be found in hadith books. All of these du'ās can be said together or individually. Other du'ās can be said with these du'ās but it is better to stick to du'ās approved by the Prophet ﷺ.

Ending the Janāzah Prayer (Fourth Takbeer)

Then the imam should say the fourth takbeer and the congregation should follow and after that the imam should say:

Arabic	اَلسَلامُ عَلَيْكُم وَرَحْمَةُ اَللهِ
Transliteration	As salāmu 'alaykum wa raḥmatullāh
Translation	Peace be on you and the mercy of Allah

turning his face to the right first and then to the left; and the congregation should do the same.

Note: Some people emphasise a lot on saying du'ās after the completion of Janāzah Prayer but we did not find a single hadith supporting this idea. Janāzah Prayer is designed so that all the du'ās a person wants to say for the deceased can be said after the third takbeer. This was the authentic practice of Prophet Muhammad ﷺ and his Companions.

PRAYER DURING A JOURNEY

Islam is a practical way of life and considers the situations in which its followers may face difficulties. So, Allah ﷻ has made the things easy for the believers in some situations. Included in the facilities is the permission for shortening and combining daily prayers during a journey.

Qasr Prayer (Short Prayer)

When a Muslim is on a journey, they should pray two rak'ahs fard for Ẓuhr, 'Asr and 'Isha. Fajr and Maghrib prayers remain as they are.

It is More Rewarding to Pray a Qasr Prayer (Short Prayer)

It is more rewarding to pray a qasr prayer while on a journey.

Evidence
The Messenger of Allah ﷺ said: "It is a gift from Allah which he has bestowed upon you, so you should accept it." (Muslim)

Combining Prayers

A person on a journey can combine Ẓuhr and 'Asr prayers together, praying them both at Ẓuhr or 'Asr time. They can also combine Maghrib and 'Isha prayers together praying them both at Maghrib or at 'Isha time.

Evidence
Ibn Abbas ﷺ says that the Messenger of Allah ﷺ used to combine Ẓuhr and 'Asr together when he was on a journey and also, he used to combine Maghrib and 'Isha. (Bukhari)
Mu'adh ﷺ says that the Messenger of Allah ﷺ was on a journey for the Battle of Tabuk. If the sun had already declined when he wanted to start his journey after having camped somewhere, he would combine his Ẓuhr and 'Asr prayers together and pray them both at Ẓuhr time, and if he decided to move before the sun had declined then, he delayed the Ẓuhr prayer and prayed it combined with 'Asr prayer at 'Asr time. And if the sun had already set when he wanted to move, he would combine Maghrib and 'Isha together at Maghrib time. And if the sun had not set when he wanted to move, he would delay Maghrib and pray it with 'Isha at 'Isha time. (Abu Dawud and Tirmidhi)

These hadiths are very clear in their meaning and prove that combining prayers while on a journey is a proven and regular practice of Prophet Muhammad ﷺ. Still there are people who do not believe in combining prayers together while they are travelling. However, this is a gift from Allah ﷻ which the believers should accept gratefully and if someone wants to reject Allah's and his Messenger's offer it is up to them.

When to Shorten and Combine Prayers

Now there is the question as to what is the limiting distance and the duration of the journey to make the facility of qasr and jama valid.

Evidence
Yahya bin Yazeed said: "I asked Anas bin Malik ﷺ when the qasr prayer was allowed?" Anas ﷺ answered that the Messenger of Allah ﷺ whenever he went away about three miles, he prayed qasr. (Muslim, Ahmad, Abu Dawud and Baihaqi)

Evidence
Abu Sa'id ؓ said that whenever Rasulallah ﷺ travelled about one farsakh (approximately three miles) he would pray qasr. (Talkhees Ibn Hajr)

On the basis of these hadiths, a person can pray qasr and can combine prayers when the distance he travels away from home is three miles. This distance is the minimum limit for qasr prayer. However, there are many varied opinions on the minimum limit of the distance; for example, nine miles, forty-eight miles or one day's journey. In our opinion, the correct definition of a journey is what society as a whole recognises under their circumstances. Currently, the majority of scholars are of the view that the distance at which a traveller may join prayers is forty-eight miles.

Duration of Journey

A person can pray qasr and combine their prayers for as long as they remain on a journey, whether it takes weeks, months or years. Even if they stay put in one place to fulfil the purpose of their journey, they can continue to pray qasr and combine the prayers. However, if they intended to stay in a place for a fixed number of days then the opinions differ on how long they can go on combining and shortening the prayers.

After a careful study of hadiths, we can say that when someone stays in a fixed place temporarily, they can be considered a traveller on a journey, and there is no limit on the number of days they can pray qasr and combine their prayers.

Nafl Prayer on a Journey

The Prophet ﷺ always offered Witr prayer during his journey and he emphasised and expressed the importance of two rak'ah sunnah of the Fajr prayer. Therefore, the believers should pray these while on a journey.

But what about any other nafl and sunnah prayers? The following hadith answers this question.

Evidence
Hafs bin Asim says: "I accompanied Abdullah bin Umar ﷺ on a journey to Makkah. On the way to Makkah, he led us in the Ẓuhr prayer and offered two rak'ahs. Then he went to sit in his tent. He saw some people praying and asked me what they were doing. 'They are praying nafl,' I said. Then he said, 'If I could pray nafl then I should have prayed the complete fard prayer.' Then he continued, 'I accompanied the Messenger of Allah on a journey. He did not pray during his travels more than two rak'ahs. Then I accompanied Abu Bakr, Umar and Uthman and they did the same as Prophet Muhammad ﷺ.' There is a good example for you in the practice of Prophet Muhammad ﷺ." (Bukhari)

There are some other hadiths which prove that some of the Companions used to pray nafls during their journey. It is better not to pray nafls while travelling but if you stay somewhere and have time, you may do so.

NOTES